WILLIAM & MARY

By The Sea

First Printing

*A collection of seafood recipes and revelations compiled by
the Society of the Alumni and the Virginia Institute of Marine Science
of the College of William & Mary in Virginia.*

Cookbook

Cover Artist Martin Barry

King and Queen Press
The Society of the Alumni
The College of William and Mary in Virginia

First Printing   5,000 copies   September, 1997

ISBN 0-9615670-7-4
Library of Congress Catalog Card Number: 97-73499

Printed in the USA by

WIMMER
The Wimmer Companies
Memphis

The William and Mary Alumni Center

TABLE OF CONTENTS

THE SOCIETY OF THE ALUMNI

The College of William and Mary

William and Mary By The Sea, a collaborative effort between the Society of the Alumni and the Virginia Institute of Marine Science, is just one example of how the Alumni Society works to bring new and unique products, programs and services to William and Mary's alumni, parents, students, faculty and friends.

From its modest beginnings on July 4, 1842, the Society of the Alumni has grown to more than 100,000 alumni and friends around the nation and the world. That network, which brings together the graduates of the College and its current faculty, staff, students, parents and friends, has grown into a thriving, award-winning organization.

The Society is the sixth oldest alumni association in the nation and as part of its mission conducts and sponsors homecoming weekend festivities, class reunions, more than 60 worldwide chapter and club programs, many constituent associations, a full-fledged travel program, and continuing education opportunities such as Alumni College and the Academic Festival. The Society brings together alumni working on behalf of the Admission Office, alumni and prospective students, and career advisers with soon-to-be graduates, publishes the *Alumni Gazette* and *The William and Mary Magazine* and recognizes outstanding achievements by alumni, faculty, students and coaches with a host of awards, scholarships and internships. Through the Society, alumni can purchase William and Mary products and clothing in the Alumni Gift Shop, enjoy valuable member benefit programs and use the Alumni Center for private events.

The Society sponsors an engaging variety of special events on and off campus, including the New York Auction, hosted by its New York Chapter; Senior Spring Day, to welcome graduating seniors into the ranks of alumni; Olde Guarde Day, in honor of the College's most senior alumni; and Student Host Weekend, to give high school students an opportunity to experience campus life. The association is administered by an executive vice president and is governed by a corporate board of 15 directors.

Perhaps most significantly, the Society keeps tabs on the growing number of alumni — where they are and what they do — and keeps them in touch with each other and the College. Alumni play a necessary role in maintaining the vitality of the College through their enthusiastic support as mentors and keepers of tradition and knowledge.

Now alumni truly have a place to call home when they return to campus. The newly expanded William and Mary Alumni Center, dedicated during Homecoming 1997, stands to serve alumni and friends worldwide. This beautiful state-of-the-art facility will be the showcase for many alumni events — from a small, intimate dinner to our annual Homecoming celebration. The Alumni Center is a careful adaptation of the existing historic building that preserves the warmth and grace of the original house. Leadership Hall, the centerpiece of the Center, provides a splendid view of the Walter J. Zable Stadium and is graced by the spacious Ukrop Terrace. Central to the design is the utilization of the verdant hillside lawn site with terraces, plazas and a William and Mary family courtyard nestled beneath trees.

As we continue to develop the strong partnership between the College and its alumni, it is our hope that you enjoy this cookbook, and the various other products that are available to you through the Society of the Alumni. *Bon appétit!*

For more information on the Society of the Alumni please call 757/221-1842 or visit our site on the World Wide Web at: http://www.wm.edu/alumni

The Society represents alumni of one of the nation's most historic and beautiful colleges.

THE VIRGINIA INSTITUTE OF MARINE SCIENCE

The College of William and Mary

The School of Marine Science is one of five graduate schools of the College of William and Mary. Chartered in 1940, the Virginia Institute of Marine Science/School of Marine Science (VIMS/SMS) has a tripartite mission of research, education and advisory service in marine science. The role of the Institute is to provide sound scientific research that contributes to new knowledge, and to provide accurate, reliable data upon which policy makers and regulatory agencies can base stewardship decisions. VIMS/SMS is the largest marine center in the nation focused on coastal ocean and estuarine research. The Institute is recognized nationally and internationally as a world leader in marine science.

The 35-acre main campus, located in Gloucester Point at the mouth of the York River, offers easy access to Virginia's estuaries, tidal and non-tidal wetlands as well as the Chesapeake Bay and Atlantic Ocean. The Institute is well equipped with state-of-the-art field and laboratory equipment to support advanced research in numerous disciplines such as: geochemistry, physical oceanography, genetics, immunology and pathobiology. This includes a recirculating flume, a mass spectrometry lab, an automated DNA sequencer and instrumentation for benthic boundary layer research. Instrument fabrication equipment and calibration tanks for various sensors enable scientists to engineer, develop and maintain specialized research equipment. Facilities include six buildings with flow-through salt water systems.

The Eastern Shore Laboratory (ESL), located in Wachapreague, is surrounded by embayments, salt marshes, barrier beaches and coastal waters. Facilities include wet and dry labs for visiting scientists, a seawater flume and dormitory space for 40 visitors. Widely recognized for its contributions to bivalve aquaculture, the ESL is also the primary site for oyster reef restoration research. Both campuses provide rich, living laboratories for research and teaching. Four hundred and fifty scientists, students, and support staff are engaged in activities supporting the mission of the Institute.

The comprehensive research plan includes the Core Research program. These programs are designed to evolve and change to meet new objectives and issues as they arise. All core programs are interdisciplinary and involve multiple departments. Scientists from various disciplines provide research to support different aspects of each program. VIMS defines core research on the basis of issues or problems rather than by department or discipline. Aquaculture is one of the Core Research Programs. Vital contributions are provided from program research in benthic processes, species biology, nutritional research, nonnative species, disease processes, microbial biology, coastal management and policy, and economics. Computational modeling plays a role in all core programs. Through mathematical models, scientists are able to calculate outcomes that may result under specific conditions. Currently, VIMS has 11 Core Research Programs.

Both masters and doctoral degrees are awarded by the school. Currently, 120 students are enrolled-approximately half in masters programs and half in doctoral programs. Students are drawn from colleges and universities nation-wide. International students compose 12 percent of the student body. All students take a series of core courses designed to provide a broad base of fundamental knowledge in marine science. Academic programs are closely allied with the research and advisory activities. Candidates must complete a research based thesis or dissertation. Graduates find work in research, education, management and regulatory agencies at the local, state and federal level as well as in the corporate and private sectors.

Research and academic programs are based in five departments: biological sciences, environmental sciences, fisheries science, physical sciences, and resource management and policy. Interdisciplinary research focuses on increasing fundamental knowledge of the various processes affecting marine environments, and seeking practical solutions to current issues. Within each department, scientists from related disciplines maintain programs that support departmental objectives. Program research focuses on areas such as disease in fish and shellfish, plankton and nutrient processes, ecology of various marine plants and animals, processes of sediment fate and transfer, water quality, shoreline processes and structures, wave dynamics and marine geology and geochemistry. This diversity reflects the varied expertise of the scientific staff.

The issues are global and require thorough understanding in order to manage regional, national and international impacts.

- Fifty percent of the world's population live in the coastal zone. It is predicted that by 2010, 75 percent of all Americans will live within 50 miles of a coast.

- Approximately 90 percent of the world's fish catch comes from the coastal ocean.

- Land-based activities profoundly influence coastal ocean and estuarine waters.

- Coastal waters respond rapidly to events such as storms and the effects extend through all or most of the water column.

- Estuarine waters provide spawning areas and nursery habitats to many species of marine life.

For additional information on the Virginia Institute of Marine Science
please call: 804/684-7000 or 804/684-7011

Visit our site on the World Wide Web at: http://www.vims.edu

ABOUT THE ARTIST

Martin Barry, a lifelong resident of Baltimore, Md. is one of the East Coast's most well-respected pen, ink and water color artists. His portfolio of more than 150 hand-watercolored limited edition prints depicts numerous points of interest primarily along the Eastern Seaboard. Included are scenes of Boston, New York, Philadelphia, Baltimore, Washington, D.C., Williamsburg, Richmond, Norfolk and Atlanta. He is currently in the process of depicting scenes in other areas.

Barry's works are included in many important collections throughout the world. Most recently, his rendition of The Cathedral in Baltimore was chosen by the Vatican for a special issue commemorative stamp. His works can also be found in the archives of the Jimmy Carter Library, the Vatican, Johns Hopkins University, Baltimore City Hall and the Apostolic Delegation in Washington, D.C. Barry was also commissioned by the governor of Maryland for an original work as the state's gift to the Republic of China.

A graduate of Loyola College, he attended the Maryland Institute of Art and the Schuler School of Fine Art. The family studio in the Baltimore suburb of Towson includes Barry, his wife Barbara, two daughters, Barbara and Leigh, a son Martin III and two sisters, Anne Downey and Carol Miller.

To obtain information on Martin Barry's complete selection of prints, please call 410/879-3334.

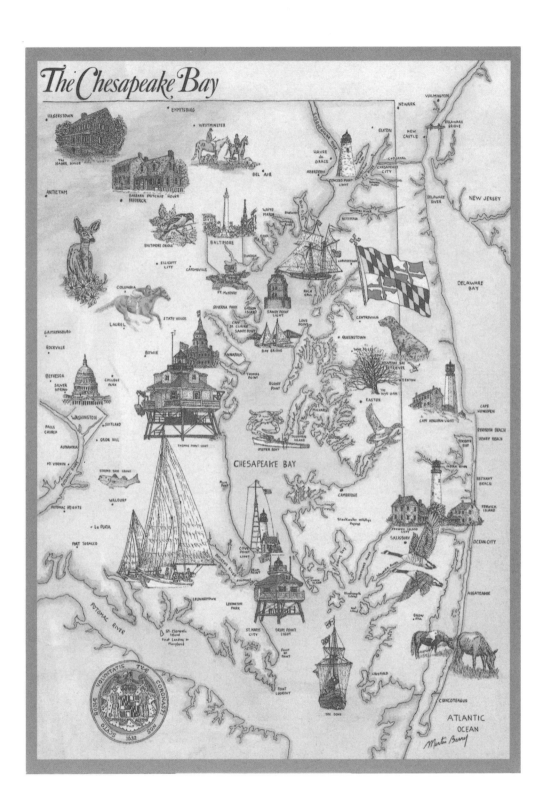

Crab

CRAB

There are many different species of crabs, but in the Chesapeake Bay region, there is only one which matters: the blue crab. *Callinectes sapidus*, the "beautiful swimmer" has been the symbol of the Bay region for hundreds of years. The blue crab is the key ingredient in many a favorite Tidewater seafood recipe. They are steamed by the bushel for summer picnics, or their succulent meat is simmered in soups, folded into dips and stuffed into fish.

The blue crab is native to the eastern Atlantic and Gulf coasts, but it has been introduced to both the Mediterranean and the Pacific. The Chesapeake Bay, however, is the major blue crab producing area of the world. Hardshell blue crabs are sold live, whole steamed or as picked meat which is fresh, frozen or pasteurized. Crabs purchased live should show movement; discard any which do not. Picked meat should be kept very cold and used within two days.

SOFT-SHELLS: A CHESAPEAKE DELICACY

The molting process, which occurs regularly in the life of all crustaceans, is of particular significance in the blue crab. It is this phenomenon which supplies us with the highly prized soft-shell crab, which can be eaten shell, legs and all. Watermen can detect a crab which is close to molting by checking for subtle color changes on the edge of the crab's swimming leg. Crabs which are harvested just before they shed are held in large, shallow trays of water where they are carefully watched. Each crab must be removed as soon as it sheds, before its shell begins to harden and before it is eaten by the other crabs in the tray. The live soft-shell crabs are carefully packed and shipped out immediately. Soft-shells are often frozen, making them available year-round. Japan, Canada and Britain are three of the largest importers of Chesapeake Bay soft-shell crabs.

Appetizer

Stonewall Vineyards' Cayuga Crab Dip

1	tablespoon finely chopped onion	½	cup (2 ounces) shredded Cheddar cheese
2	tablespoons olive oil	1	(6½-ounce) can crabmeat, drained, and bits of shell removed
½	cup milk		
1	tablespoon lemon juice		
3	tablespoons Cayuga white wine	⅓	cup sliced almonds

Sauté onion in a large skillet in hot oil over low heat 1 to 2 minutes. Slowly stir in milk, and bring to boil. Add lemon juice, wine, and cheese, stirring until cheese melts. Add crabmeat. Spoon into an ovenproof serving dish. Top with almonds. Broil 6 inches from heat (with electric oven door partially open) 5 minutes or until bubbly. Serve hot with crackers or pieces of French bread.

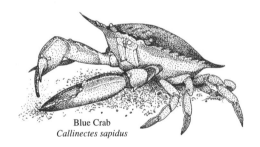

Blue Crab
Callinectes sapidus

Appetizer

Crab Mousse

7	ounces cream cheese	1	can crabmeat, drained (or 1 pound fresh crabmeat), and bits of shell removed
1	small onion, chopped		
1	(10¾-ounce) can cream of mushroom soup		
1	envelope unflavored gelatin	¾	cup mayonnaise
¼	cup water	½	teaspoon curry powder

Cook cream cheese in a medium saucepan over medium heat until thoroughly heated. Stir in onion, soup, gelatin, and water. Remove from heat. Add crabmeat, mayonnaise, and curry powder. Pour into a mold, and chill until set. Serve with crackers or sliced French bread.

Yield: 3 cups.

Shellfish is not a scientific term, but in seafood terminology it refers to animals known to scientists as crustaceans (crabs, shrimp, lobsters and crayfish), mollusks (oysters, clams, scallops, mussels, snails), and cephalopods (squid and octopus). All of these organisms are invertebrates, many of which have tough protective shells on the outside of their bodies rather than an internal skeleton.

Appetizer

Hot Crab Casserole Hors d'oeuvre for Chafing Dish

1	cup cooked white rice
½	pound backfin crabmeat, bits of shell removed
5	hard-cooked eggs, finely chopped
1½	cups mayonnaise
½	teaspoon salt
½	teaspoon white pepper
	Dash of black pepper
6	ounces evaporated milk
4	ounces cream cheese (softened)

Combine rice, crabmeat, and chopped egg in a large bowl. Stir in mayonnaise, salt, white and black pepper, milk, and cream cheese. Pour mixture into a ½-quart baking dish. Bake at 350° for 20 minutes. Pour mixture into a chafing dish, and serve with Melba toast or croustades. Two iced-tea spoons (not sterling silver) are perfect serving utensils.

Yield: 30 servings.

This is also delicious over toast points at brunch; serves 12 generously.

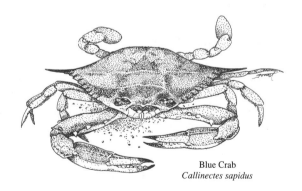

Blue Crab
Callinectes sapidus

Appetizer

Hot Crabmeat Canapé

1 (8-ounce) package cream
    cheese, softened
1 tablespoon milk
2 tablespoons finely chopped
    onion
½ teaspoon creamed horseradish

1 (6½-ounce) can crabmeat,
    drained, and bits of shell
    removed
    Dash of pepper
½ cup sliced almonds, toasted
    Paprika

Stir together first 6 ingredients. Pour mixture into a 9-inch pie plate or shell-shaped baking dish. Top with almonds. Bake at 350° for 15 minutes. Sprinkle with paprika. Serve hot with crackers, cocktail rye bread, or celery and cucumber boats.

Yield: 6 to 8 servings.

Blue Crab

Appetizer

Crab Meltaways

1   package English muffins
1   (6½-ounce) can crabmeat, rinsed, drained, and bits of shell removed
½   cup butter or margarine, softened
1   (7-ounce) jar sharp process Cheddar cheese spread
2   tablespoons mayonnaise
½   teaspoon seasoned salt
½   teaspoon garlic salt

Split muffins, and slice each half into 4 pieces; arrange on a baking sheet. Combine crabmeat and remaining ingredients, and spread on each muffin piece. Freeze at least 30 minutes. Remove from freezer; broil 6 inches from heat (with electric oven door partially open) until puffy, bubbly and golden brown. Serve hot.

Yield: 48 servings.

**Can be stored in the freezer
in zip-top plastic bags.**

Appetizer

Eastern Shore Crabmeat Hors d'oeuvre

2	cups half-and-half		Dash of hot sauce
½	cup butter or margarine	1	pound backfin crabmeat,
¼	cup all-purpose flour		bits of shell removed
	Dash of onion salt	½	cup dry sherry

Cook half-and-half and butter in top of a double boiler over medium-low heat until butter melts. Stir in flour, and cook until mixture thickens to a sauce. Add onion salt, hot sauce, crabmeat, and sherry. Cook, stirring often, until thickened. Pour mixture into a chafing dish, and serve with crackers or Melba toast.

Yield: 24 servings.

This recipe can be made a day ahead and reheated.

Blue Crab

Appetizer

Crab Cakes with Creole Mustard Sauce

1   cup mayonnaise
2   large egg yolks
2   tablespoons dry mustard
2   tablespoons chopped fresh tarragon (1 teaspoon dried)
2   teaspoons Worcestershire sauce
1   teaspoon seafood seasoning or Creole seasoning
¼   teaspoon hot sauce
¼   teaspoon salt
¼   teaspoon pepper
2   pounds lump crabmeat, bits of shell removed
3   cups fresh breadcrumbs
    Vegetable oil
    Creole Mustard Sauce

Combine first 9 ingredients; stir in crabmeat. Spread breadcrumbs on 2 baking sheets. Drop crabmeat mixture by tablespoonfuls on top of breadcrumbs. Shape into small cakes, and roll into crumbs to coat evenly. Transfer cakes to a wax paper-lined baking sheet. Chill. Heat ½ inch vegetable oil in a 12-inch skillet over medium heat. Cook crab cakes in batches of 4 for 2 to 3 minutes on each side. Drain on paper towels. Reheat cooked cakes on a baking sheet at 375° for 15 to 20 minutes. Arrange on a warm serving platter; add dollop of Creole Mustard Sauce to each crab cake.

CREOLE MUSTARD SAUCE:

1   cup mayonnaise
1   jalapeño pepper, seeded and minced (or 5 drops hot sauce)
½   red bell pepper, finely chopped
3   tablespoons Dijon mustard
2   tablespoons finely chopped chives

Combine all ingredients in a bowl. Makes 1½ cups.

Yield: 4 dozen.

Soup/Stew

Crabmeat Gumbo

2	onions, chopped	⅓	teaspoon dried fennel
1	green bell pepper, chopped	⅓	teaspoon seasoned salt
2	tablespoons vegetable oil	⅓	teaspoon cayenne pepper
½	garlic clove, minced	1	tablespoon Worcestershire sauce
1	package frozen okra		
1	(20-ounce) can tomatoes	2	cups clam juice
3	tablespoons tomato puree	10	cups water
1	teaspoon dried thyme	2	cups cooked white rice
1	bay leaf	1	pound lump crabmeat, bits of shell removed
⅓	teaspoon dried basil		

Sauté onion and bell pepper in hot oil in a large stockpot until tender; add next 13 ingredients, and simmer, uncovered, 1 hour. Add rice and crabmeat. Simmer 5 to 10 minutes.

Yield: 8 to 10 servings.

Shedding Crab

How cold is your refrigerator? Check the temperature at several levels to find the coldest spot.

Seafood should be kept chilled between 32 and 40 degrees.

Kirk's Crabby Creamy Red Pepper Soup

4   **large red bell peppers, cored and seeded**
4   **cups whipping cream**
2   **cups cooked crabmeat**
     Sea salt to taste

Place bell peppers in a large stockpot; add cream. Cook over medium-low heat until soft. Pour mixture into a blender; process until pureed. Return pepper mixture to stockpot; add crabmeat, and season with sea salt. Cook until thoroughly heated. Serve with spinach salad and toasted cheese squares.

Yield: 4 servings.

Seasoning with sea salt makes the difference!

Preparing Crab for Market

Casserole

Crab Casserole

3	cups croutons	1	teaspoon dry mustard
²⁄₃	pound crabmeat, bits of shell removed	¼	teaspoon onion salt
1²⁄₃	cups shredded Cheddar cheese	¼	teaspoon salt
6	eggs	¼	teaspoon pepper
3	cups milk	5	bacon slices, cooked and crumbled

Grease a 9 x 13-inch baking dish; sprinkle croutons to cover bottom of dish. Layer crabmeat and then cheese over croutons. In a bowl, beat eggs and next 5 ingredients together. Pour mixture over cheese. Bake 325° for 45 minutes. Top with bacon, and bake 5 to 10 more minutes. Serve with salad and fresh bread.

Yield: 6 servings.

Great for a luncheon.

Main Dish

Crab Imperial

1   **cup sour cream**
2   **tablespoons mayonnaise**
     Dash of salt
     Dash of pepper
     Dash of hot sauce
1   **pound backfin lump crabmeat**
4-6 **crab-shaped shells or ramekins**
2   **tablespoons butter or margarine,**
     cut up
     Paprika

Stir together first 5 ingredients. Stir in crabmeat. Fill shells or ramekins. Dot with butter, and sprinkle with paprika. Bake at 250° for 30 minutes or until bubbly. Serve with twice-baked potatoes, a green salad, or coleslaw.

Yield: 4 servings.

FENWICK ISLAND LIGHTHOUSE, DEL.

Main Dish

Crab Imperial

1	pound backfin or lump crabmeat, bits of shell removed	1	tablespoon butter or margarine
½	teaspoon salt	⅓	cup milk
½	teaspoon pepper		Dash of salt and pepper
1	teaspoon dry mustard	1	egg, beaten
	Dash of lemon juice	3	tablespoons mayonnaise, divided
1	teaspoon chopped fresh parsley		Paprika
1	tablespoon all-purpose flour		

Gently stir together first 6 ingredients in a large bowl; set aside. Cook flour, butter, milk, salt, and pepper in a small saucepan over medium-low heat, stirring constantly, until thickened. Cool sauce. Stir egg and 2 tablespoons mayonnaise into sauce; add to crab mixture, being careful not to break up lumps of crabmeat. Spoon crab mixture into greased shell-shaped baking dishes (4 to 6 depending on size). Cover and chill several hours or overnight. Just before baking, spread on each a thin layer of remaining 1 tablespoon mayonnaise; sprinkle with paprika. Place on a baking sheet. Bake at 400° for 20 to 25 minutes. For a casual dinner, serve with French fries and coleslaw. For a more elegant meal, serve with a baked potato and fresh English peas.

Yield: 4 to 6 servings.

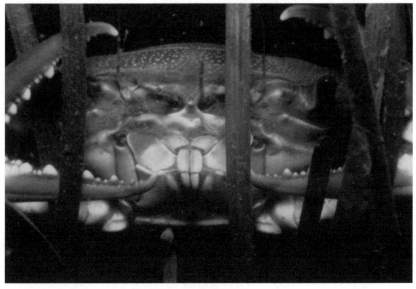

Blue Crab

Main Dish

Crab-Spinach Soufflé

1	(12-ounce) package frozen spinach soufflé, thawed
32	ounces small-curd cottage cheese
6	tablespoons all-purpose flour
6	eggs, beaten
½	cup butter or margarine, cubed
½	pound shredded sharp Cheddar cheese
1	(6½-ounce) can crabmeat, drained, (or ½ pound fresh crabmeat) and bits of shell removed

Combine all ingredients in a greased 13 x 9-inch pan. Bake at 350° for 1 hour.

Yield: 12 to 16 servings.

**If using a glass baking dish,
reduce cooking time by 10 to 15 minutes.**

Seafood

Sunset

Main Dish

Creamed Crabmeat

2	tablespoons butter or margarine	1	teaspoon sherry
2	tablespoons all-purpose flour	1	teaspoon grated onion
1	cup milk	1	tablespoon chopped red and green bell pepper
	Dash of celery salt	1	pound backfin crabmeat, bits of shell removed
½	teaspoon Worcestershire sauce		

Melt butter in a heavy saucepan over low heat. Add flour, and stir 3 to 4 minutes until well blended and the taste of the flour has vanished. Slowly stir milk into butter mixture. Add celery salt and next 4 ingredients. Simmer, whisking constantly, until thick, smooth, and thoroughly heated. Add crabmeat just as sauce thickens. For a creamier dish, use about half as much sauce as there are solids.

Yield: 4 servings.

**Serve in sterilized scallop shell, and top with
shredded sharp Cheddar cheese. Heat under broiler.**

Main Dish

Crab-Stuffed Chicken

6	chicken breast halves, skinned and boned
	Dash of salt
	Dash of pepper
½	cup chopped onion
½	cup chopped celery
3	tablespoons butter or margarine
3	tablespoons dry white wine
8	ounces crabmeat, drained, and bits of shell removed
½	cup herb-seasoned stuffing
2	tablespoons all-purpose flour
½	teaspoon paprika
2	tablespoons butter or margarine, melted
1	envelope Hollandaise sauce mix (or prepare your own)
¾	cup milk
2	tablespoons dry white wine
½	cup (2 ounces) shredded Swiss cheese

Flatten chicken to ¼-inch thickness using a meat mallet; sprinkle with salt and pepper, and set aside. Sauté onion and celery in 3 tablespoons butter in a skillet until tender. Remove from heat, and add wine, crabmeat, and stuffing. Toss to blend. Divide crabmeat mixture into 6 equal portions, and spoon over chicken breasts. Roll up, jellyroll fashion, and secure with a toothpick. Combine flour and paprika; rub over rolled chicken breasts. Place rolls in a 7 x 12-inch baking dish, and drizzle with 2 tablespoons melted butter. Bake at 375° for 1 hour or until chicken is done. Do not overbake chicken. Transfer to a serving platter. Combine Hollandaise mix and milk in a saucepan; whisk over medium heat until thickened. Add wine and cheese, and cook, whisking constantly, until cheese melts. Pour some sauce over chicken, and pass sauce at the table. Serve with wild rice and greens with vinaigrette dressing, marinated vegetables, or a fruit salad.

Yield: 6 servings.

Main Dish

Deviled Crab Cakes

Juice of ½ lemon
2 tablespoons mayonnaise
1 tablespoon mustard
1 egg, beaten
½ teaspoon hot sauce
1 teaspoon Worcestershire sauce

2 slices bread (crusts removed), crumbled
Dash of salt
Dash of pepper
1 pound lump crabmeat, bits of shell removed

Combine first 9 ingredients. Add crabmeat, stirring lightly; shape into 6 to 8 crab cakes. Place on baking sheets. Bake at 350° for 25 to 30 minutes or until golden brown.

Yield: 6 servings.

Seafood

Main Dish

Crab Cakes with Homemade Tartar Sauce

1	pound fresh lump crabmeat, bits of shell removed
½	teaspoon prepared mustard
1	tablespoon minced green onions
1½	teaspoons minced red bell pepper or sweet banana pepper
½	cup breadcrumbs
2	teaspoons baking powder
½	teaspoon Worcestershire sauce
5	tablespoons mayonnaise
1	egg, beaten
	Vegetable shortening

TARTAR SAUCE:

1	tablespoon capers, drained and chopped
1	tablespoon sweet pickle relish or chopped dill pickles
1	tablespoon chopped fresh parsley
1	teaspoon chopped green onions
1	cup mayonnaise
1	teaspoon lemon juice
	Dash of salt and pepper

Combine first 8 ingredients; stir in egg, and gently shape by ¼-cupfuls into cakes. Heat shortening in a deep skillet over medium-high heat until hot. Fry crab cakes until brown. Drain on a paper towel, and keep warm. Stir together capers and remaining ingredients, and serve cold with warm crab cakes.

Yield: 4 servings.

> *Crabmeat must be fresh for this recipe.*
> *Serve with sliced tomato on lettuce with*
> *butterbeans or succotash.*

Main Dish

Texas Crab Cakes

⅓ cup thinly sliced green onions (green part only)	2 tablespoons diced yellow bell pepper
1 cup plus 2 tablespoons clarified butter, divided	1 pound fresh white bread (high-quality loaf bread)
1 pound fresh lump crabmeat, bits of shell removed	1 large egg, beaten
2 tablespoons diced red bell pepper	2 tablespoons whipping cream
	1½ teaspoons chopped fresh marjoram

Wilt the green onions for 1 minute in 2 tablespoons butter. Place crabmeat in a bowl, breaking up any lumps. Add the green onions and diced peppers. Remove crusts from bread, and make breadcrumbs of the bread. Add egg, ½ cup breadcrumbs, cream, and marjoram to crab mixture; mix together by hand. Shape into 8 cakes, about ¾-inch thick and 2½ inches wide. Lightly press more breadcrumbs onto each side of patties, and chill if not cooking immediately. Heat remaining 1 cup butter in a large, heavy saucepan so that crab cakes sizzle when put in pan. Cook at low heat 5 minutes on 1 side and 3 minutes on the other. Crab cakes should be golden but not brown. Serve with jalapeño sauce, hush puppies, and a side salad.

Yield: 4 servings.

Main Dish

Olga's Maryland Crab Cakes

1	slice soft white bread, crusts removed
1	egg, beaten
½	cup mayonnaise
½	cup loosely packed chopped fresh parsley
½	teaspoon dry mustard
1	teaspoon Worcestershire sauce
1	teaspoon seafood seasoning
1	pound backfin or lump crabmeat, bits of shell removed
	Vegetable oil

Tear (do not cut) bread into small pieces. Combine egg and next 5 ingredients in a large bowl; stir well. Stir in bread pieces. Gently fold in crabmeat until evenly distributed, being careful not to break up lumps of crabmeat. Shape crabmeat mixture by ¼ cupfuls into cakes. Pour oil to a depth of ¼ inch into a large, heavy skillet. Heat oil over medium-high heat. Fry crab cakes 4 to 5 minutes on each side (turning gently) or until golden brown. Drain on a paper towel. Serve warm.

Yield: 4 servings.

> **The secret to these cakes is to use
> mostly crabmeat and just enough filler
> to hold the crabmeat together.**

Main Dish

Hot Steamed Crabs

1	cup vinegar	Coarse salt to taste
1	cup beer	Seafood seasoning to taste
½	bushel crabs	

Place vinegar and beer in bottom of a crab steamer. Position rack, then place a layer of live crabs on rack. Crabs are fast and their claws can grip and cut; use thick gloves and tongs when handling. Cover crabs with a layer of course salt and seafood seasoning. Place another layer of crabs on top, followed by more salt and seafood seasoning. Continue layering until pot is filled. Cut a gasket out of newspaper to cover pot; cover with lid. This retains steam better. Place pot on stove; cook over high heat 20 to 25 minutes or until crab shells are bright red. Serve immediately. Cover the table with oil cloth topped with old newspaper or brown paper to absorb juices from the crabs and to dispose of shells later. Use mallets to crack the shells and knives to get out the meat. Store leftover crabs in refrigerator up to 1 day. The secret of this recipe is to serve crabs hot with lots of spicy seafood seasoning. Serve with ice-cold beer.

Yield: ½ bushel.

> *Steamed crabs are best cooked in a tall crab steamer, with a rack,*
> *that can hold up to 48 medium-size crabs. Buy them by the bushel and*
> *steam 2 to 3 pots, one after the other. You can get any amount you want,*
> *but they are usually sold by the dozen or bushel. The cost of crabs varies*
> *greatly depending on abundance each season. You may pay anywhere*
> *from $35 to $85 a bushel. Chesapeake Bay blue crabs are the best.*
> *Make sure all the crabs you buy are alive; they will move!*
> *Crabs are more lively at room temperature.*
> *Do not allow crabs to come into direct contact with ice;*
> *fresh water will kill them. Do not cook dead crabs.*
> *The rule is, if in doubt, throw them out.*

Main Dish

Mock Crab Enchiladas

1   (10¾-ounce) can condensed cream of chicken or cream of spinach soup
½   onion, chopped
3   dashes hot sauce
2   dashes black pepper
12 ounces frozen chopped spinach, thawed and drained
8   ounces imitation crabmeat
2   cups (8 ounces) shredded Monterey Jack cheese, divided
10 flour tortillas
1   cup milk

Stir together first 4 ingredients. Divide mixture in half, placing in 2 separate bowls (1 bowl should be large enough to combine remaining ingredients). In larger bowl, stir in spinach, crabmeat, and 1 cup cheese. Place ⅓ cup crab mixture into each tortilla. Roll up, and place, seam side down, in a greased rectangular baking dish. Add milk to smaller bowl of soup mixture; pour over enchiladas. Bake at 350° for 15 minutes. Sprinkle remaining 1 cup cheese over top; bake 10 more minutes.

Yield: 5 servings.

Main Dish

Crab-and-Peach Quesadillas

1	medium shallot, finely chopped	¼	teaspoon dried savory
3	tablespoons chopped green chiles (green bell pepper or jalapeño may be substituted)		Dash of hot sauce
			Dash of salt
1	teaspoon minced garlic	1	cup (4 ounces) finely shredded Muenster cheese
1	teaspoon olive oil	½	cup (2 ounces) finely shredded Monterey Jack cheese
¼	pound backfin crabmeat, bits of shell removed	½	cup (2 ounces) finely shredded Longhorn or Colby cheese
2	ripe peaches, peeled and chopped (roughly ⅓-inch cubes)		Vegetable cooking spray
¼	teaspoon dried oregano leaves	12	(10-inch) flour tortillas

Sauté shallot, chiles, and garlic in hot oil in a skillet until shallot is translucent, about 2 minutes. Add crabmeat; cook 3 minutes or until thoroughly heated and liquid is absorbed. Take special care to leave crab lumps as intact as possible. Remove from heat; transfer to a nonmetal bowl. Add peaches and next 4 ingredients. Chill 30 minutes. Combine cheeses in a separate bowl. Heat a griddle (or large sauté pan) over medium heat. Grease with cooking spray. Place 1 tortilla on griddle. Spread one-sixth of crab mixture evenly over tortilla; immediately sprinkle with cheeses. As cheese melts, top with another tortilla, and spray with cooking spray. Cook about 2 minutes or until cheese melts. Turn to brown the other side. Remove to a cutting board; cut into wedges using a pizza wheel, and serve immediately. A simple green salsa and herbed sour cream are excellent accompaniments.

Yield: 4 servings.

> *The amount of heat can be adjusted by adding extra minced jalapeño,*
> *which certainly makes for conversation. Quesadillas can be served*
> *all at once by placing them on a warm platter in oven until all*
> *are finished. Serve as soon as last quesadilla is cooked.*

Main Dish

Crabmeat as Served to His Royal Highness, The Prince of Wales

1	pound lump crabmeat
1	cup grated cheddar cheese
1	small jar capers, drained
1-2	teaspoons pimiento
¼	cup mayonnaise

Preheat oven to 350°. Carefully pick through crab to remove all shell; set aside. In a separate bowl, mix all remaining ingredients using only enough mayonnaise to hold mixture together. Very gently, fold in crabmeat; do not stir. Bake 20-30 minutes or until mixture is heated through and cheese melts.

Yield: 4-6 servings.

*Reprinted from
The William & Mary Cookbook, © 1993*

Main Dish

Sautéed Soft-Shell Crabs

Household scissors
6   prime velvet soft-shell crabs
1   cup all-purpose flour on a plate
    for dredging

Canola oil
Clarified butter

SEASONING SAUCE:
3   tablespoons lemon juice
3   tablespoons clarified butter

¼   teaspoon chopped fresh parsley

Clean the crabs as soon as you get them. To do so hold the scissors in one hand and a crab in the other, its stomach resting on your palm, its claws dangling over the sides of your hand. Snip off the head and eyes. Lift up a side wing of the top shell; cut off the finger-like gills attached to the body on each side. Note that the little blobs of stored fat located under the wings should be left on. Lift up the apron and snip off. Squeeze the center of the crab to force out the sand sack and the tomalley (greenish matter). Place the cleaned crabs stomach-side up on a plate, so the backs will stay moist. Although you may clean the crabs somewhat ahead and refrigerate them, they are at their best when cooked as soon as possible. To cook the crabs, heat a large cast iron pan over medium heat. Dredge soft-shell crabs in flour and shake off excess. When pan is hot, add ½ canola oil and ½ clarified butter to ¼ inch deep. Lay crabs in pan, backside down. Stand back as the crabs cook, for they tend to explode! When the crabs brown lightly, turn and finish cooking on the other side. Total cooking time is approximately two minutes. Remove the crabs and keep them warm as you sauté the rest, adding more butter and oil as needed. In a small bowl, stir together 3 tablespoons each of lemon juice and clarified butter, brush it over the crabs, and sprinkle with a touch of chopped parsley. Serve immediately.

Yield: 6 servings.

Soft-Shell Crab Dinner

Shrimp

SHRIMP

The most popular shellfish in the United States is shrimp. More than half the shrimp sold in the United States is aquacultured, raised in ponds in Central and South America and Asia. Three types of wild shrimp - the pink, white, and brown - are commercially harvested along the Atlantic coast of the United States, with a large portion coming from the southeast Atlantic and the Gulf of Mexico. Commercial species of shrimp occasionally are found in the Chesapeake Bay, but not in great enough numbers to support a fishery.

Shrimp are omnivores, exploring the bottom with their long flexible antennae for anything edible. They will feed on all types of organic debris, plants, and small animals. For protection, they cling to plants and often burrow into the sand or mud.

To cook raw shrimp, steam them or immerse them in boiling water (add salt and other seasonings to taste) just until they turn pink and the flesh is opaque rather than transparent. This should take no longer than 3 - 8 minutes, depending on the size and the amount of shrimp. Shrimp can also be broiled, grilled, baked, stir-fried, sautéed or deep-fried. They can be served hot or cold, but if they are reheated, be careful not to overcook them or they will toughen. Freeze raw shrimp with the shell on (remove the head) for better flavor. Shrimp heads and shells can be used to make seafood stock.

Appetizer

Seaside Shrimp Dip

1	(8-ounce) package cream cheese, softened	⅛	cup ketchup
¼	medium onion, grated	1	tablespoon Worcestershire sauce
	Dash of hot sauce	1	pound cooked, peeled, deveined shrimp, chopped
3	tablespoons lemon juice		
⅓	cup mayonnaise		

Stir first 7 ingredients together until smooth. Add shrimp, and chill 1 hour. Serve with crackers, bagel chips, or raw vegetables.

Yield: 2 cups.

Soup/Stew

Spicy Black Bean Soup with Shrimp

2	cups dried black beans, rinsed
3	tablespoons butter or margarine
2	tablespoons vegetable oil, divided
2	cups finely chopped onion
4	garlic cloves, minced
2	teaspoons minced fresh ginger
½	medium jalapeño pepper, minced
1	(28-ounce) can plum tomatoes, drained and coarsely chopped
2	teaspoons dried thyme
6-8	cups chicken stock
2	teaspoons salt
½	teaspoon pepper
24	medium shrimp, peeled and deveined
1½	cups plain yogurt
2	garlic cloves, minced
	Fresh cilantro leaves

Soak beans in water to cover in a heavy pot at room temperature overnight. Drain and rinse beans; set aside. In a large stockpot, heat butter and 1 tablespoon oil over medium heat. Add onion, garlic, ginger, and jalapeño. Sauté 5 minutes or until tender. Add beans, tomato, thyme, and 6 cups stock. Bring to a boil. Reduce heat, cover, and simmer 2 to 2½ hours or until beans are tender. Add more stock as necessary during cooking time. Transfer half of bean mixture to a food processor; process until pureed. Return puree to remaining bean mixture. Add salt and pepper. Cover and keep warm. Heat remaining 1 tablespoon oil in a skillet over medium heat; add shrimp and sauté 3 minutes or until shrimp turn pink. Ladle soup into 6 serving bowls. Stir together yogurt and minced garlic. Garnish each serving with 4 shrimp, a dollop of yogurt mixture, and a few cilantro leaves. Serve with sourdough bread, green salad, and a full-bodied red wine. Wonderful on a chilly day.

Yield: 6 servings.

Pasta/Salad

Seafood Delight: Shrimp with Linguine

³/₄ cup olive oil
¼ cup fresh parsley, chopped
⅓ cup white wine vinegar
1 teaspoon dried oregano
1½ teaspoons dried basil
½ teaspoon garlic salt
½ teaspoon pepper
1 pound linguine, cooked and drained

1½ pounds shrimp, cooked, peeled, and deveined
½ pound snow pea pods, blanched and stringed
6 scallions, chopped
4 medium tomatoes, peeled and chopped

Combine first 7 ingredients in a large serving bowl. Add linguine, and toss. Combine shrimp, snow peas, scallions, and tomato. Add to linguine mixture; toss gently. Cover and chill at least 2 hours. Serve with Virginia ham biscuits and fresh fruit.

Yield: 10 servings.

Salad

Broccoli-Shrimp Salad

1	cup mayonnaise
⅓	cup sugar
2	tablespoons white wine vinegar
1½	teaspoons curry powder
3	cups broccoli florets, chopped
⅔	cup chopped celery
6-8	minced green onion tops
1	cup halved seedless grapes
2	cups peeled, cooked, deveined shrimp

Stir together first 4 ingredients. Toss in broccoli and next 3 ingredients. Chill 1 hour. Add shrimp just before serving. Serve with heated mini croissants.

Yield: 4 servings.

Fishing Pier in Mathews County

Main Dish

Low Country Boil or Frogmore Stew

3	new potatoes per person (optional)	1	teaspoon ground black pepper per 4 pounds shrimp
1	teaspoon vinegar per pound of shrimp	½	pound cooked smoked sausage per person
½	teaspoon hot sauce per pound of shrimp	2	onions per person (optional)
1	teaspoon ground red pepper per 4 pounds of shrimp	1	ear shucked corn per person
		½	pound unpeeled shrimp per person

Fill a large stockpot three-fourths full of water. Add potatoes and next 4 ingredients; bring to a boil, and cook 5 minutes. Add sausage, and return to a boil; cook 5 minutes. Add onions, and boil 5 minutes. Add corn, and boil 5 minutes. Check all ingredients for doneness, especially potatoes. Add shrimp, and boil until shells begin to separate. Turn off heat and let stand for a few minutes. Drain and serve.

It works well to cover a table with newspaper or
brown paper when working with the shrimp and the corn.
Instead of doing dishes, just roll up the paper and throw it away.

Main Dish

Spicy Shrimp

½   **cup olive oil**
2   **tablespoons Creole seasoning**
3   **tablespoons fresh lemon juice**
2   **to 3 tablespoons chopped fresh parsley**
1   **tablespoon honey**
1   **tablespoon soy sauce**
⅛   **teaspoon cayenne pepper or to taste**
1   **pound peeled, deveined uncooked large shrimp**

Combine first 7 ingredients in a 9 x 13-inch baking dish. Add shrimp, and toss to coat. Chill at least 1 hour. Bake at 350° 8 to 10 minutes or until shrimp are done. Garnish with a twist of lemon and/or minced parsley. Serve with couscous and steamed vegetables or crusty bread and a salad of baby greens with lemon vinaigrette.

Yield: 4 servings.

Main Dish

Butterflied Shrimp

1   package Italian salad dressing mix
1   tablespoon minced green bell pepper
¼   cup minced onion
½   garlic clove, minced

⅔   cup vegetable oil
2   tablespoons lemon juice
⅔   cup dry white wine
1   pound uncooked shrimp, deveined

Stir together first 7 ingredients in a shallow pan. Add shrimp, tossing to coat; chill at least 2 hours. Broil shrimp 4 inches from heat (with electric oven door partially open) 2 minutes. Turn and broil 2 more minutes. Serve with heated marinade or cocktail sauce. Serve over thin pasta with a green salad and French bread.

Yield: 4 servings.

Main Dish

Shrimp Curry

1	package crab boil
1½	quarts water
1	tablespoon salt
3	oranges, juiced with some peeling
3	lemons, juiced with some peeling
2	pounds unpeeled shrimp, heads removed
4	tablespoons all-purpose flour
4	tablespoons curry powder
1	teaspoon salt
½	teaspoon cayenne pepper
¼	teaspoon ground cinnamon
1	egg, beaten
½	cup butter or margarine, melted
2	cans fruit cocktail, undrained
1	cup milk

Bring first 3 ingredients to a boil; boil 10 minutes. Add orange and lemon juice and peelings. Add shrimp, and return to a boil. Remove from heat and let cool; peel shrimp, and cut into pieces. Reserve ¼ cup shrimp stock. Combine flour and next 4 ingredients in a bowl. Gradually add egg, melted butter, and fruit cocktail. Transfer flour mixture to top of a double boiler; whisk in milk. Add ⅛ cup reserved shrimp stock, stirring until sauce reaches a nice consistency. Add more shrimp stock if sauce becomes too thick. Stir in shrimp, and serve over rice with the following condiments: chutney, toasted coconut, chopped green bell pepper, drained crushed pineapple, chopped cucumber, chopped peanuts, bacon bits, French fried onion rings, chopped preserved ginger, chopped avocado, chopped hardcooked egg, fine ground coffee, chopped apple, chopped tomato, and finely diced orange peel. Each person is served rice and sauce and a little from each condiment dish.

Yield: 4-6 servings.

Main Dish

Roasted Garlic Shrimp

½	cup extra virgin olive oil		Dash of hot sauce
½	cup peanut oil		Dash of white Worcestershire
4	garlic cloves, minced		sauce
1	teaspoon garlic salt	1	pound unpeeled large shrimp,
¾	teaspoon garlic powder	½	pound paper-thin sliced
⅓	teaspoon ground white pepper		prosciutto

Combine first 8 ingredients in a large, nonmetal bowl. Whisk until salt is dissolved. Remove legs from shrimp, and rinse shrimp. Using a serrated knife (some steak knives work well), cut through top of shrimp shells and approximately one-third of the way into shrimp meat. The serrated knife should help remove veins by simply wiping onto a towel. Keep shells as intact as possible. Add shrimp to oil mixture. Chill 30 to 60 minutes. Light a covered grill with a very moderate amount of charcoal or hardwood. Once the coals are reduced to 50 percent of their original size, spread them to the sides, away from direct heat. Soaked smoking chips may be added just prior to cooking shrimp. Line a grill basket with a single layer of prosciutto. Arrange shrimp in a single layer over prosciutto; cover with another single layer of prosciutto before replacing grill basket cover. Place in center of grill, and cover with grill lid. Cook until shrimp turn pink, about 4 minutes. Carefully flip grill basket; cover and cook 3 more minutes. Serve shrimp and prosciutto immediately as a main course. Great with summer salads (cucumber and ginger slaw or Southwest corn salad) or ratatouille.

Yield: 2 to 4 servings.

The unpeeled method is added insurance for moist shrimp.
This recipe can be cooked without shells with a little extra care.
Done in this way, the cooked shrimp can be chilled and served with a lime
salsa or crushed tomatoes with fresh basil. Can also be used as an appetizer.

Main Dish

Shrimp au Gratin

1	pound shrimp, cooked, peeled, and deveined
1	(4-ounce) jar sliced mushrooms (or 8-ounce package sliced fresh mushrooms, sautéed in butter)
3	tablespoons butter or margarine
3	tablespoons chopped onion
1	cup (4 ounces) shredded sharp Cheddar cheese (or ½ cup grated Romano cheese plus ½ cup shredded sharp Cheddar)
¼	teaspoon salt
1½	cups milk
¼	cup all-purpose flour
¼	teaspoon dry mustard
	Dash of pepper
2-3	tablespoons dry white wine

Layer shrimp and mushrooms in a baking dish. Melt butter in a skillet over medium heat; sauté onion until tender. Combine ¾ cup cheese and next 6 ingredients in a saucepan; cook over medium-low heat, stirring constantly, until mixture forms a white sauce. Pour over shrimp and mushrooms; sprinkle with remaining ¼ cup cheese. Bake at 375° for 10 minutes. Serve alone or on rice or pasta.

Yield: 4 to 5 servings.

Main Dish

Shrimp, Leeks, and Sun-Dried Tomatoes Over Pasta

1	teaspoon olive oil	1	pound fusille, rotini, or other nonlinear pasta
1/8	teaspoon sea salt		
2	medium leeks, sliced into rings and separated	8	dried tomatoes packed in oil, drained and sliced, oil reserved
4	garlic cloves, thinly sliced	4	tablespoons capers, rinsed
1	tablespoon unsalted Spike	1½	pounds uncooked, peeled, deveined shrimp
2	tablespoons dried oregano		
1/4	cup Chardonnay or other dry white wine	1	tablespoon fresh oregano leaves

Prepare to cook pasta by bringing a large pot of water to a boil, adding olive oil and sea salt. Coat a large skillet with vegetable cooking spray, and add 1 teaspoon oil reserved from tomatoes. Cook over medium heat until hot; add leeks, garlic, Spike, and dried oregano. Slowly add Chardonnay, adding a little more if leek mixture sticks to skillet. Continue to cook over medium heat. Add pasta to boiling water, cooking until al dente. Add tomatoes and capers to leek mixture. Several minutes before pasta is done, add shrimp and oregano leaves to leek mixture; continue to cook over high heat until shrimp turn pink. Drain pasta, and spoon into warm pasta bowls. Top with sauce, and garnish each bowl with a sprig of fresh oregano. Serve with chilled Chardonnay and fresh crusty bread.

Yield: 4 servings.

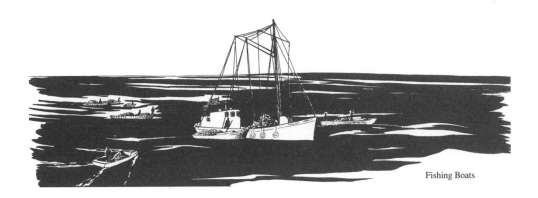

Fishing Boats

Main Dish

Shrimp Fra Diavolo with Fusilli

3	tablespoons olive oil
¾	pound shrimp, peeled and deveined
¼	teaspoon crushed red pepper
½	teaspoon salt
⅓	cup white wine
1	cup chopped onion
2	teaspoons minced garlic
1	(28-ounce) can whole tomatoes, cut in pieces
1	pound fusille or penne pasta, cooked
¼	cup chopped fresh parsley

Heat 1 tablespoon oil in a large skillet. Add shrimp, red pepper, and salt. Sauté 1 minute or until shrimp are opaque. Add wine. Boil 30 seconds. Transfer to a bowl. Heat remaining 2 tablespoons oil in skillet. Add onion, and sauté 6 to 7 minutes or until translucent. Stir in garlic and tomato. Bring to boil; boil 5 minutes. Stir in shrimp. Cook 1 minute. Toss with fusille and parsley.

Yield: 5 to 6 servings.

Main Dish

Linguine Salad

1	pound linguine, cooked		4	teaspoons prepared mustard
1	pound small shrimp cooked, peeled, and chilled		1	teaspoon celery seed
			¼	teaspoon pepper
2	cups mayonnaise		3	cups sliced celery
2	tablespoons cider or wine vinegar		1	cup sliced green onions
			1	cup sliced radishes
3	teaspoons salt		2	tablespoons parsley, chopped

Combine linguine and shrimp in a large serving bowl. Add mayonnaise and next 5 ingredients. Toss until well mixed; add celery and remaining ingredients. Make the day before or early in the day and chill until ready to serve.

Yield: 6 servings.

The Chickadee

Main Dish

Shrimp Scampi Mediterranean

1	ounce olive oil
1½	pounds shrimp, peeled and deveined
1	garlic clove, chopped
1½	cups white wine
1	green bell pepper, chopped
1	yellow bell pepper, chopped
1	red bell pepper, chopped
1	purple onion, chopped
1	tomato, chopped
1	ounce pimiento-stuffed olives, chopped
1	ounce ripe black olives, chopped
½	bunch chopped parsley
1	zucchini, chopped
1	fresh lemon
	Dash of salt
	Dash of pepper
2	tablespoons butter or margarine

Heat olive oil in a 12-inch sauté pan over medium heat. Add shrimp, garlic and white wine. Sauté 1 to 2 minutes or until shrimp turn pink. Add peppers, onion, and next 5 ingredients. Sauté 2 to 3 minutes. Reduce heat, and add a splash of lemon juice, salt, and pepper to taste. Fold in butter until mixture is a creamy texture. Serve over pasta or rice.

Yield: 4 servings.

This recipe can be adjusted with a hint of cream to make it a little smoother or crushed red pepper to give it zest.

Main Dish

Shrimp and Angel Hair Pasta

1½ garlic cloves, chopped
2 tablespoons diced yellow bell pepper
2 dried tomatoes, drained and cut into julienne strips
½ cup broccoli florets
4 tablespoons olive oil
5 ounces shrimp, peeled and deveined

2 tablespoons white wine
1 tablespoon fresh lemon juice
1½ tablespoons fresh basil leaves
1 cup cooked angel hair pasta
Parmesan cheese
Freshly ground black pepper to taste

Sauté first 4 ingredients in hot oil in a skillet about 2 minutes. Add shrimp; sauté 2 to 3 more minutes. Add wine, lemon juice, and basil. When shrimp turns pink, add pasta; toss well. Sprinkle with Parmesan cheese and/or freshly ground black pepper.

Yield: 2 servings.

Sorting and Weighing Fish

Main Dish

President's House Angel Hair Pasta with Shrimp

1/3-1/2	cup extra-virgin olive oil
4	cloves garlic, minced
1 1/2-2	pounds large shrimp, peeled and cleaned
1	cup dry white wine
2	ripe tomatoes, peeled, seeded and diced
2	tablespoons minced fresh basil
1/4	teaspoon salt
1/8	teaspoon freshly ground black pepper
2	cups heavy cream
3	tablespoons butter
1 1/2	pounds fresh angel hair pasta, cooked al dente

GARNISH:

6-8	tablespoons freshly grated Romano cheese
6-8	sprigs fresh basil

Sauté garlic in olive oil; add shrimp and cook, stirring constantly, for 1-2 minutes, or until shrimp begin to turn pink. Add wine and next 5 ingredients; cook over medium heat for 3 minutes or until shrimp are just cooked. Remove shrimp from pan and set aside. Continue cooking sauce until reduced in volume and sauce coats the back of a spoon. Whisk in butter; stir until smooth. Toss well-drained pasta and shrimp in sauce; heat through. Spoon onto individual serving plates and garnish with cheese and fresh basil.

Yield: 6 servings.

An elegant dish.

Reprinted from
The William & Mary Cookbook, © 1993

Main Dish

Baked Shrimp with Feta Cheese

2	medium onions, thinly sliced
½	cup extra-virgin olive oil
2	pounds tomatoes, peeled and coarsely chopped
1-2	teaspoons finely minced parsley
½	teaspoon salt
¼	teaspoon freshly ground pepper
2	cloves garlic, minced
2	pounds large uncooked shrimp, peeled and cleaned
½	pound Greek feta cheese
	Parsley, for garnish

Sauté onions in olive oil until tender; add tomatoes, parsley, salt, pepper and garlic. Cover and simmer for 30-40 minutes, stirring occasionally. Put sauce and shrimp in 6 individual ovenproof dishes. Crumble feta cheese over shrimp and bake uncovered in a preheated 450° oven for 10-15 minutes, or until shrimp are cooked and cheese is melted. Garnish with parsley and serve hot.

Yield: 6 servings.

Good for buffet dinner parties.

Reprinted from
The William & Mary Cookbook, © 1993

BODIE ISLAND LIGHTHOUSE

Main Dish

Michelob Shrimp - As Served at Kingsmill-on-the-James

1	cup sifted flour
2	tablespoons Hungarian sweet paprika
1	tablespoon seafood seasoning
1	teaspoon salt
½	teaspoon dry mustard
1	(12-ounce) bottle Michelob beer
2	pounds large (21-35 count) shrimp, peeled, deveined, tail intact
	Additional flour for dusting shrimp
3	cups hot cooking oil
	Salt to taste
	Pepper to taste

ORANGE MARMALADE SAUCE:

1	cup orange marmalade
1	cup bottled chili sauce
¼	cup bottled prepared horseradish

In a medium bowl, sift together the first 5 batter ingredients. Add beer, mixing well. Dust shrimp lightly with flour, then dip in batter, coating each well. Deep-fry (375°) until shrimp are golden brown, about 2 to 3 minutes. Drain between sheets of absorbent paper. Season with salt and pepper to taste and serve with Orange Marmalade Sauce. To make Orange Marmalade Sauce combine all ingredients, blending well.

Yield: 6 servings.

Shrimp at their best!

Reprinted from
The William & Mary Cookbook, © 1993

Fish

FISH

Fish has always been a staple in the Chesapeake Bay cuisine, due to its availability and the seasonal variety of species. Today, local seafood markets are stocked not only with native Bay fish but also with an array of fish, wild and farmed, from around the world. Whether the catch of the day comes from your own hook and line or from the seafood counter, fresh fish can be a regular item on your home menu.

BLACK SEA BASS

This grayish-black fish with spiny fins is caught near oyster beds, rocks and submerged wrecks. It is a hardy fish which is shipped live to ethnic markets in northern cities. It is popular fried and steamed whole in Chinese cuisine. The firm, tender white flesh is delicious baked and served with creamy sauces. Market size ranges from 1 to 3 pounds. For an attractive presentation, leave the black and silver skin on the fillets and serve them skin side up.

BLUEFISH

This torpedo-shaped, bluish-silver fish is known as a ferocious predator and a spirited fighter when hooked. Bluefish follow migratory schools of menhaden and other bait fish up and down the Atlantic coast, resulting in a plentiful supply of fresh blues in the spring and fall of most years. People who believe them to be too strong and "fishy" tasting have probably never eaten a well-prepared, fresh bluefish. Clean bluefish immediately after they are caught and keep them very cold until you are ready to prepare them. Their rich taste and high fat content make bluefish an excellent choice for grilling, broiling or smoking.

CODFISH

Atlantic cod are rarely inhabitants of the Chesapeake Bay, but they are common in supermarkets, usually sold as frozen fillets. Cod, haddock and pollack are all members of the codfish family. Cod are found in cold waters from Virginia north to the Arctic. Their flaky, mild, white meat can be prepared in many different ways, but if you choose to grill it, use a grilling basket or foil wrap to keep the large flakes from falling apart when cooked.

CROAKER

The croaker ranges from the Chesapeake Bay to the Gulf of Mexico and is a popular Bay sportfish. Their name comes from the croaking noise they make by contracting muscles near their swim bladder. Market size is 1 to 4 pounds. The croaker's mild, flaky, lean meat is good for pan frying, baking, broiling or steaming.

FLOUNDER

Flounder belongs to the large family of flatfish which includes halibut, turbot, soles and dabs. These fish are remarkable for the transformation they undergo from a tiny juvenile fish which swims upright like other fish, to a flat, thin fish which swims on its side. During this change, the fish's skull twists until both eyes are on one side of its head, with the eyed side facing up. The flounder spends most of its time buried in the sand waiting for prey. Flounder fillets are thin and should be cooked carefully for a short time, just until the meat begins to flake. Don't overwhelm the flounder's delicate flavor with strong-tasting sauces. Flounder stuffed with crabmeat is an elegant and popular dish.

ROCKFISH AND HYBRID STRIPED BASS

The Chesapeake's declining population of rockfish, or wild striped bass, made a successful comeback after a fishing moratorium was placed on the species in the 1980's. Rockfish are anadromous, meaning they migrate from saltwater into fresh and brackish water to spawn. The striped bass often found in seafood markets today is an aquacultured hybrid between the wild rockfish and a white bass which lives in both fresh and brackish water. The hybrid striped bass is shorter and thicker than the wild species. The black longitudinal stripes on the hybrid's sides appear broken into several segments, where the wild rockfish has unbroken stripes.

Striped bass are mild-tasting, firm and flaky. The farm-raised hybrids are marketed at about two pounds, so they are ideal for baking whole. Most any other cooking method will do as well. Leave the skin on to make the most of its delicate flavor and attractive appearance.

ATLANTIC SALMON

Before dams and water pollution spoiled many of its spawning grounds, the Atlantic salmon was a plentiful fish along the coast of New England. Now, due to its success as a farm-raised species, the Atlantic salmon has once again become a popular and widely available food fish. It is farmed in many countries, including the United States, Canada, Norway, Ireland and Chile. The pink color of a salmon's flesh is due to a carotenoid pigment from the insects and crustaceans it feeds upon. This color is obtained in farmed fish by adding color to their feed. Atlantic salmon is slightly oily but has a mild flavor. It is available whole, in steaks and fillets, and is especially popular smoked.

AMERICAN SHAD

Springtime in the Chesapeake is marked by the annual shad run, when these anadromous fish swim up into Tidewater rivers and creeks to spawn. Native Americans harvested these plentiful fish and depended on smoked shad to help sustain them through the winter. George Washington is said to have been fond of baked shad. Shad were so abundant that they were used as fertilizer in the early 1800's, but the population began to decline due to overfishing, water pollution, and the damming of streams. Today, some of the barricades to the shad's upstream migration are being removed in an effort to reopen the historic spawning grounds.

The shad's rich-flavored flesh makes it worth the trouble it takes to pick through its notorious maze of thin bones. Leave the skin on to help keep the delicate meat intact. Shad is sold whole or filleted, and is delicious baked, broiled or sautéed. The traditional way to cook shad is to place it on an oiled wooden plank and cook it in a slow oven or in front of an open fire. The female shad is considered to be the better flavored, and its rich roe is a sought-after delicacy which can be broiled or fried.

SPOT

Anyone who has fished the Chesapeake is bound to have caught one of these familiar fish. Spot swim in schools and are often caught in large numbers when they are running. They are named for the dark spot located just behind each gill. Spot are small and make an excellent panfish.

TUNA

Tuna are streamlined, powerful fish, many of which migrate great distances in the open ocean. They are prized as game fish for their speed, size and fighting qualities. They feed on squid and schools of fish. Several different species are commercially harvested for seafood.

Although most tuna in the United States is sold canned, fresh and frozen tuna steaks and loins are available year-round. Tuna is a firm, meaty fish, sometimes compared to beef in appearance when it is raw. The dark-colored flesh turns light when it is cooked. It should not be overcooked or it will be dry, tough and tasteless. Cook it medium-rare for the best color, texture and flavor. It is good baked, broiled or grilled.

Appetizer

Ted Peters' Famous Smoked-Fish Spread

2	cups finely diced onion	1¼	quarts mayonnaise
1	cup finely diced celery	3½	quarts deboned, flaked smoked
1½	cups sweet pickle relish with pimiento		fish (mullet preferred)

Combine all ingredients, stirring well. Chill and serve. Best if served 2 to 3 days after preparation.

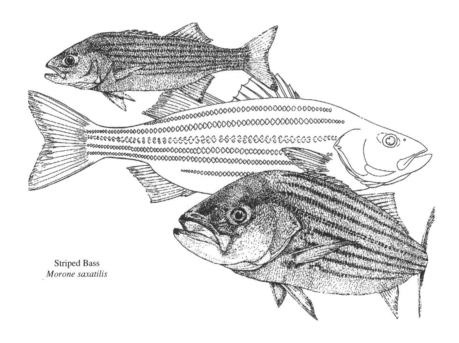

Striped Bass
Morone saxatilis

In Florida, this dish is a big hit at William and Mary alumni functions.

Appetizer

Marinated Bass

3	pounds bass fillets
½	cup celery tops
1	teaspoon salt
1-1½	ounces pickling spices
	Cheese cloth
1-2	green peppers, cut into bite-size pieces
2	cups chopped green onions with tops, or 2 cups chopped sweet onions

MARINADE:

2½	cups salad oil
1	cup white vinegar
2-3	lemons, juiced
5	tablespoons celery seed
1-2	teaspoons salt
1	package Good Season's dry salad dressing, Italian or garlic
2-3	shakes hot sauce

Place bass in pan and cover with water; add celery tops and 1 teaspoon salt. Tie pickling spices in cheese cloth and add to water. Bring to boil; reduce heat to low and simmer until fish flakes easily when touched with a fork. Strain and let cool. Remove any bones and skin. In a large crockery or glass bowl, alternate layers of fish, green peppers and onions; pour marinade over all. To make marinade mix all ingredients and stir. Cover and chill for at least 12 hours or up to a week. Gently stir occasionally.

Yield: 24-30 servings.

Serving suggestion: partially drain and serve cold with assorted crackers.

Reprinted from The William & Mary Cookbook, © 1993

Appetizer

Salmon Mousse

2	envelopes unflavored gelatin	1	tablespoon lemon juice
½	cup cold water	16	ounces canned salmon
1	cup boiling water	½	cup chopped onion
16	ounces sour cream	1	teaspoon fresh dillweed
¾	cup Thousand Island dressing		

In a large bowl, sprinkle unflavored gelatin over cold water; let stand 1 minute. Add boiling water, and stir until gelatin is dissolved. Add sour cream, dressing, and lemon juice; stir until smooth. Add remaining ingredients; process in a food processor or blender until smooth and creamy. Grease a 6-cup fish-shaped or other mold with vegetable cooking spray; pour in mousse. Chill until set. Garnish with fresh dill.

Yield: 6 cups.

Appetizer

Chilled Smoked Fish with Horseradish Sauce

1	whole redfish
	Garlic salt
	Lemon-pepper seasoning
	Juice of 3 lemons
½	cup butter or margarine, melted
2	tablespoons Worcestershire sauce
	Dash of hot sauce
1	teaspoon parsley, chopped

HORSERADISH SAUCE:

2	cups sour cream
1	tablespoon prepared horseradish
2	teaspoons lemon juice
¼	teaspoon lemon-pepper seasoning
	Dash of salt
1	tablespoon chopped chives
1	teaspoon fresh dill
	Paprika

Sprinkle fish with garlic salt and lemon-pepper. Combine lemon juice, melted butter, Worcestershire, hot sauce, and parsley; set mixture aside. Place aluminum foil over tail and head of fish. Smoke fish over low fire in a covered grill for about an hour, basting every 15 minutes, or until fish flakes easily with a fork. Hickory chips should be used to get smoky flavor.

Combine sour cream and next 6 ingredients; spoon into a serving bowl. Sprinkle with paprika.

Yield: 2 cups.

If you don't feel like smoking your own fish, Tony's Smoke House and Cannery in Oregon City, Oregon, can do the job for you. Call 1-800-755-6885. Tony's smoked Chinook salmon is fantastic. This is a great dish for parties.

Soup/Stew

Oven Fish Chowder

2	pounds flaked cod or haddock	4	whole cloves
4	potatoes, peeled and sliced	1/4	cup butter or margarine
3	onions, sliced	1/4	teaspoon dill seed
1	garlic clove, peeled and crushed	1/2	cup dry white wine or vermouth
1	bay leaf	2	cups boiling water
3	sprigs fresh celery leaves	2	cups sour cream
2½	teaspoons salt		

Put first 12 ingredients into a 3-quart baking dish. Bake, covered, at 375° for 1 hour. Remove and discard celery leaves, bay leaf, and cloves. Mix in sour cream, and break up fish. Cook 10 more minutes or until thoroughly heated.

Yield: 8 to 10 servings.

Abandoned Fishing Boat

Soup/Stew

Smoky Chowder

2	onions, chopped
1	tablespoon vegetable oil
6	cups fish stock (or 3 cups water plus 3 cups clam juice)
1	cup white wine
1½	pounds peeled, diced potatoes
½	teaspoon salt
1	tablespoon fresh parsley, chopped
1	tablespoon fresh thyme (or 1 teaspoon dried)
2	bay leaves
1	whole smoked trout, salmon, or other fish (remove skin and bones and break into chunks)
1	cup milk
1	cup light cream
1	teaspoon lemon juice
	Dash of pepper
	Dash of hot sauce
1	tablespoon fresh parsley for garnish

Sauté onion in hot oil over medium heat in a large stockpot until translucent. Add fish stock and next 6 ingredients. Simmer 20 minutes or until potato is done. Add trout, milk, and cream; simmer gently. (Do not boil or the cream will curdle.) Stir in lemon juice, pepper, and hot sauce to taste. Garnish with parsley.

Yield: 4 servings.

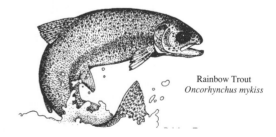

Rainbow Trout
Oncorhynchus mykiss

This is even better than New England codfish chowder! The chowder can be made ahead of time, but wait to add the trout and lemon juice until after the chowder is reheated.

Main Dish

Broiled Salmon

2	tablespoons butter	2	tablespoons dark brown sugar
1	tablespoon dry sherry	¾	to 1 pound fresh salmon steak
1	tablespoon soy sauce		

Melt butter in a broiler pan. Stir sherry, soy sauce, and sugar into melted butter; add salmon to mixture, and chill about 1 hour, turning salmon every 15 minutes. Broil 6 inches from heat (with electric oven door partially open) 5 to 7 minutes on each side. Serve with chilled Chardonnay.

Yield: 2 servings.

Main Dish

Creamed Salmon and Peas

1	tablespoon of butter or margarine		Salt and pepper to taste
1	tablespoon all-purpose flour	1	cup flaked salmon (fresh or canned)
1	cup whole milk	1	cup English peas, cooked

Cook butter, flour, and milk in a saucepan over medium-low heat, stirring constantly, until mixture creates a nice cream sauce. Season to taste. Add salmon and peas, and cook until thoroughly heated. Serve hot on toast halves. This is a great luncheon dish with asparagus or a green salad.

Yield: 4 servings.

Main Dish

Salmon Lasagna

3	tablespoons vegetable oil
¼	cup all-purpose flour
3	cups milk
¼	cup grated Parmesan cheese
½	teaspoon white pepper
2	(9 ounce) packages frozen creamed spinach, thawed
1	pound mozzarella cheese, shredded
1	(15-ounce) container cottage cheese
1	(8-ounce) package lasagna noodles, cooked and drained
1	(14- to 15-ounce) can salmon, flaked
1	tomato, chopped

Heat oil in a 2-quart saucepan over medium heat. Stir in flour, and cook, stirring constantly, 1 minute. Stir in milk; stir until thickened. Stir in Parmesan cheese and pepper. Set sauce mixture aside. Mix thawed spinach, mozzarella cheese, and cottage cheese. Spread half of sauce in bottom of a 9 x 13-inch glass baking dish. Arrange one-third of noodles over sauce. Spoon half of spinach mixture over noodles. Place one-half of salmon over spinach mixture. Repeat noodle, spinach, and salmon layers. Top with remaining noodles and sauce. Bake, covered, at 375° for 40 minutes. Uncover and bake 15 more minutes. Sprinkle with tomato. Serve with garden salad and Italian bread.

Yield: 8 servings.

Black Drum

Main Dish

Salmon Fillets With Ginger and Peppers

3	medium-size pickled jalapeño peppers, seeded	4	fresh salmon fillets (about ½ pound each), skin removed
1	(2-inch) piece fresh ginger, peeled		Dash of freshly ground pepper
			Dash of salt
2	tablespoons sesame oil	1	tablespoon all-purpose flour

Chop peppers and ginger together to form a thick, chunky paste. Sprinkle sesame oil on both sides of salmon fillets. Spread ginger paste on both sides of fillets. Sprinkle with ground black pepper. Chill fillets 1 hour. Remove ginger paste from fillets. Sprinkle fillets with salt, and dust lightly with flour. The sesame oil remaining on the fillets provides enough oil for cooking. Cook fillets in a nonstick skillet over medium heat 3 to 5 minutes on each side or just until cooked through. Great with asparagus and fettuccine.

Yield: 4 servings.

> "Bass" is a common term used to describe several different kinds of fish, including freshwater and saltwater species. For example, black sea bass, striped bass and largemouth bass all belong to different families of fish.

Main Dish

Salmon with Lemon on Linguine

¼	cup extra-virgin olive oil
½	cup thinly sliced red onions
2	cloves garlic, minced
1	teaspoon lemon zest
1-2	tablespoons fresh lemon juice
2	tablespoons chopped fresh parsley
1	(17½-ounce) can pink salmon, drained, reserving liquid
12	ounces linguine, cooked and drained
2-4	teaspoons grated Parmesan cheese

Heat oil in skillet over low heat and stir in onions. Sauté until lightly browned. Add garlic, sauté 2 minutes. Stir in lemon zest, lemon juice and parsley. Add salmon, breaking up with a fork. Stir gently. Add reserved salmon liquid. Toss with linguine. Sprinkle with Parmesan cheese and serve at once.

Yield: 4 servings.

A good, quick recipe!

Reprinted from
The William & Mary Cookbook, © 1993

Main Dish

Poached Salmon with Cucumber Sauce

6	salmon steaks or fillets	1	tablespoon margarine
3	tablespoons chopped shallots		

POACHING LIQUID:

1½	cups water	8	whole peppercorns
1	tablespoon lemon juice	3	sprigs parsley
1	Knorr-Swiss fish seasoning cube		

CUCUMBER SAUCE:

2-3	tablespoons diced cucumber, seeded	2-3	shakes hot pepper sauce
½	cup non-fat plain yogurt or fat-free sour cream	¼	teaspoon dry mustard
		¼	teaspoon fresh lime juice
		¼	teaspoon fresh dill

GARNISH:

6	cucumber slices	6	lime slices

Preheat oven to 350°. Rinse salmon; dry and set aside. Place shallots in bottom of shallow baking dish that is just large enough to accommodate salmon steaks or fillets; top with salmon and set aside. Place all poaching liquid ingredients in a saucepan; bring to boil. Reduce heat; simmer for 2 minutes and remove from heat. Strain liquid and pour over salmon; top with margarine. Cover tightly with foil, and bake approximately 15 minutes or until fish flakes easily. Remove foil; place fish on platter. Mix all ingredients for cucumber sauce together and chill until ready to serve. Spoon cucumber sauce over salmon; garnish.

Yield: 6 servings.

Serve hot or cold.

Fishery survey using seine net.

Reprinted from
The William & Mary Cookbook, © 1993

Main Dish

Aunt Anna's 4th of July Salmon Loaf

1	can salmon
½	cup breadcrumbs
½	cup milk
½	lemon, juiced (include some grated rind)
1	teaspoon butter or margarine, melted
⅓	cup butter or margarine
3	tablespoons all-purpose flour
½	teaspoon salt
⅛	teaspoon pepper
1½	cups hot water
1	teaspoon lemon juice
2	hard-cooked eggs, sliced

Stir together first 5 ingredients. Spoon into a greased 3¾ x 7½-inch pan. Bake at 350° for 35 minutes. Melt ⅙ cup butter in a small saucepan over medium heat; add flour and seasonings. Gradually add water; bring to a boil, and boil 5 minutes. Add lemon juice and remaining butter. Add eggs, stirring until blended. Serve sauce with salmon loaf, along with fresh peas, new potatoes, and a nice white wine.

Yield: 4 servings.

Salmon, fresh peas, and new potatoes on the 4th of July are as Northern New England as you can get.

When choosing a sauce, consider the fat content and flavor profile of the fish. In general, lean mild fish will taste better with a butter and cream-based sauce; richer, fatty fish do well with acidic vinaigrettes and tomato-based sauces.

Main Dish

Roasted Tuna with Mushrooms

½ **pound fresh shiitake mushrooms, sliced**
1 **tablespoon vegetable oil**
   Dash of salt
   Dash of pepper
1¼ **cups beef broth**
2-3 **green onions**
1-2 **slices fresh ginger**

1 **cup dry vermouth**
1 **tablespoon soy sauce**
2 **tablespoons fresh parsley, chopped**
2 **pounds fresh tuna or thresher shark fillets**
2 **tablespoons butter or margarine**

Brown mushrooms in hot oil in a deep skillet 2 minutes, seasoning with salt and pepper. Add broth, green onions, and ginger; boil until reduced to 3 tablespoons liquid. Add vermouth, soy sauce, and parsley; boil until mixture is reduced by half (approximately 15 minutes). Taste, season, remove ginger, and let cool. Place mushroom mixture aside. Brown tuna in 2 tablespoons butter in skillet 2 minutes. Place tuna and skillet in the oven; bake at 400° for 10 to 15 minutes for 1-inch fillets (20 minutes for 2-inch fillets). Cut fish into serving slices, and serve on bed of mushroom mixture; drizzle with sauce.

SAUCE:
½ **roasted red pepper**
1 **cup mayonnaise**
   Dash of salt

   Dash of pepper
2 **tablespoons pine nuts**
   Fresh parsley

Puree pepper in a food processor or blender. Stir in 1 cup mayonnaise. Season with salt and pepper to taste. Garnish with pine nuts and parsley.

Yield: 4 servings.

Bluefin Tuna
Thunnus thynnus

Main Dish

Peppery Tuna Semi-Sashimi

1½	pounds finest quality fresh dark tuna
1	teaspoon sesame oil
2	teaspoons coarsely ground pepper
2	teaspoons finely ground coriander
1	teaspoon very finely chopped lemon peel
4	teaspoons wasabi (sold in gourmet stores)
1	small head of frisé or other savory salad greens
2-3	tablespoons walnut oil or mustard oil
½	cup Japanese soy sauce

Heat a charcoal grill or gas grill. Cut tuna into 4 equal-size pieces at least 1½ inches thick. Brush surfaces of tuna with sesame oil; sprinkle evenly with a mixture of pepper, coriander, and lemon peel. Spread 2 teaspoons wasabi over fish. When grill is hot, quickly sear tuna on all sides (including edges) just to brown exterior, about 2 minutes each side. The interior should remain raw. Cut each piece of tuna into several thick slices. Arrange slices on a serving plate, and garnish with a handful of salad greens dressed with walnut oil. Mix remaining 2 teaspoons wasabi with soy sauce. Pour into small bowls for dipping, or spoon a little onto plate opposite the salad.

Yield: 4 servings.

Half of recipe makes a wonderful appetizer. Serve with steamed rice. Consider cucumbers (seeded) marinated in rice vinegar as an accompaniment. Serve with Zinfandel.

Main Dish

Grilled Yellowfin Tuna with Wild Mushrooms, Leeks, Seasoned Rice, and Lemon-Lime Butter

4	ounces butter or margarine, softened	4	ounces wild mushrooms
2	ounces lemon juice and grated rind	4	ounces leeks, white part only
2	ounces lime juice and grated rind	4	(4-ounce) yellowfin tuna steaks
	Vegetable cooking spray	12	ounces cooked brown rice
		8	ounces watercress
		6	ounces grapes

Process first 3 ingredients in a blender or food processor until thoroughly blended. Chill. Spray a skillet with vegetable cooking spray. Place over medium heat; cook mushrooms and leeks in skillet until tender. Cook tuna on a hot grill on both sides approximately 4 to 5 minutes. During last minute of grilling, top with lemon-lime mixture; let melt. Place rice, sautéed mushrooms and leeks, and tuna steaks on individual serving plates. Garnish with watercress and grapes. Serve with steamed baby vegetables tossed with fresh herbs.

Yield: 4 servings.

Marinating fish is a great way to add flavor, but be careful to marinate no longer than an hour or two. The delicate muscle fibers of fish protein will begin to "cook" in the presence of acid, and will become mushy if left in vinaigrettes or marinades with tomatoes or citrus.

Main Dish

Grilled Tuna Steaks with Lemon Marinade

4	(4- to 6-ounce) tuna steaks
1	tablespoon grated lemon peel
¼	cup fresh lemon juice
1	tablespoon extra virgin olive oil
1	garlic clove, minced
2	teaspoons fresh oregano, chopped, or 1 teaspoon dried oregano
¼	teaspoon freshly ground black pepper

Rinse tuna, and pat dry. Place in a shallow glass dish. Combine remaining ingredients in a sealed container, and shake until mixed. Pour over tuna; cover and chill 30 minutes. Drain tuna, discarding marinade, and place over a hot charcoal or gas fire. Grill tuna 5 minutes on each side or until the inside is completely opaque.

Yield: 4 servings.

Fresh tuna will be more moist than frozen tuna. Be sure not to overcook.

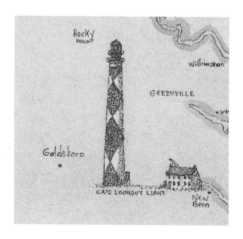

BARBARA FRITCHIE HOUSE
FREDERICK

Main Dish

Curried Tuna Casserole

6 tablespoons butter or margarine	1 tablespoon Worcestershire sauce
2 tablespoons minced shallots	Dash of salt
2 garlic cloves, minced	10 ounces small shell pasta, cooked
2 medium-size red bell peppers, cut into julienne strips	2 cups tuna, drained and flaked
4 tablespoons all-purpose flour	¼ cup dry sherry
2 tablespoons curry powder	6 saltines, crushed
3 cups hot chicken stock	2 tablespoons grated Parmesan cheese
1 cup hot milk	
½ teaspoon freshly ground black pepper	

Grease a 2-quart baking dish. Melt butter in a 2-quart saucepan; add shallots and garlic, and sauté 1 minute. Stir in pepper strips, and sauté 1 minute. Stir in flour and curry powder; cook, stirring constantly, until flour is well absorbed. Add hot stock; bring to a boil, stirring until smooth. Add hot milk, pepper, Worcestershire, and salt. Return to a boil; reduce heat, and simmer 5 minutes. Place pasta into prepared baking dish. Spread tuna evenly over pasta. Slowly pour sherry over tuna; top with warm curry sauce. Sprinkle with cracker crumbs and grated Parmesan cheese. Bake on middle shelf of oven for 30 minutes or until thoroughly heated and lightly browned on top. Serve warm.

Yield: 6 to 8 servings.

Casserole

Undergraduate Tuna Casserole

1	(7¼-ounce) package macaroni and cheese dinner
1	tablespoon margarine
¼	cup sliced celery
¼	cup chopped onion
¼	cup chopped green pepper
1	(6-ounce) can water-packed tuna, drained
1-2	tablespoons grated Parmesan cheese

Preheat oven to 350°. Cook macaroni and cheese dinner according to package directions; set aside. Melt 1 tablespoon margarine in a saucepan and sauté celery, onion and green pepper until just tender. Mix tuna and sautéed vegetables with macaroni and cheese dinner. Spoon into 2-quart casserole and top with Parmesan cheese. Bake 15-20 minutes or until casserole is completely heated.

Yield: 4 servings.

Still good after all these years!

Reprinted from
The William & Mary Cookbook, © 1993

BALTIMORE ORIOLE

Main Dish

Mock Crab Cakes

4-5	crushed saltines	1	tablespoon baking powder
1	teaspoon milk	2	tablespoons seafood seasoning
2	tablespoons mayonnaise	½	teaspoon salt
1	tablespoon chopped fresh parsley	1	egg, well beaten
1	tablespoon finely chopped celery	1	can tuna, drained and flaked

Stir together all ingredients; shape into 4 cakes. Coat a large nonstick skillet with vegetable cooking spray. Cook cakes until done. Quick-and-easy recipe for unexpected guests. Serve with coleslaw and cornbread. You can bake these cakes on a baking sheet at 350° for 20 minutes instead of frying.

Yield: 4 servings.

Buying Boat

To simply and quickly prepare a fish fillet, preheat oven to 500°. Place fillet on a buttered baking sheet. Brush with white wine and lightly season with salt and pepper. Bake for five minutes or less, depending on the thickness of the fillet. Serve with the sauce of your choice.

Summer Flounder

Main Dish

Stonewall Vineyard Flounder Vidal

1½	pounds flounder fillets
	Dash of freshly ground pepper
	Dijon mustard
2	tablespoons olive oil
½	cup Vidal Blanc wine
1	lemon

Rinse fillets, and pat dry. Sprinkle with pepper on both sides. Lightly coat both sides with mustard. Heat oil in a skillet over medium heat; add fillets, and cook until browned. Add wine; cover and simmer 3 to 5 minutes (depending on thickness). Serve with a wedge of lemon and a chilled glass of Stonewall Vineyards' Vidal Blanc.

Yield: 4 servings.

Main Dish

Flounder Fillets with Black Bean Sauce

1½ **pounds flounder fillets**	2 **tablespoons dry white wine**
3 **tablespoons vegetable oil**	2 **tablespoons soy sauce**
½ **cup coarsely diced onion**	1 **teaspoon sesame oil**
2 **tablespoons fermented black beans**	1 **teaspoon sugar**
1 **tablespoon minced garlic**	2 **teaspoons cornstarch dissolved in 1 tablespoon water**
1¼ **cups chicken stock**	

Rinse fillets, and cut into bite-size pieces. Heat oil in a wok. Stir-fry onion, black beans, and garlic. Add fish, and stir lightly. Add chicken stock and next 4 ingredients. Cover and simmer 5 minutes or until liquid is reduced by half. Stir cornstarch mixture gradually into wok; stir mixture until thickened.

Yield: 4 servings.

Netting Fish

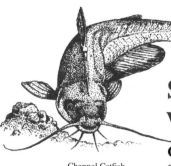

Channel Catfish
Ictalurus punctatus

Main Dish

Sesame-Crusted Fish with Orange Sauce

ORANGE SESAME SAUCE:

2	tablespoons sesame seeds, lightly toasted
2	tablespoons sesame oil
3	tablespoons minced fresh ginger
2	garlic cloves, minced
1/2	cup orange juice
1 3/4	cups chicken broth
2	tablespoons soy sauce
1	tablespoon minced orange zest
	Dash of hot sauce
1	tablespoon cornstarch dissolved in 1 tablespoon water

To toast sesame seeds, place seeds in a small skillet and heat on medium-high, stirring seeds constantly until they are just golden brown. Be careful; they burn easily! Set toasted seeds aside. Heat sesame oil in skillet over medium-high heat. Add ginger and garlic; sauté for 1 or 2 minutes. Add orange juice, chicken broth, soy sauce, orange zest, hot sauce, and toasted sesame seeds. Stir ingredients together and bring sauce to a boil. Let sauce simmer for about 10 minutes. Add the cornstarch/water mixture and stir constantly until sauce thickens.

SESAME-CRUSTED FISH:

1/2	cup sesame seeds
4	(4- to 6-ounce) firm fish fillets
1/4	cup sesame oil, divided

Roll each fillet in seeds until coated. Heat 2 tablespoons oil in a skillet over medium-high heat. Cook each fillet until nicely browned on 1 side (about 5 minutes). Add 2 tablespoons oil, 1 tablespoon at a time, as needed. Turn fillets over; cook until browned and cooked throughout (3 to 4 minutes). Serve by spooning several tablespoons of sauce onto each plate. Place fillet on top of sauce, and drizzle remaining sauce over fillets. Serve with basmati rice and stir-fried carrots, zucchini, and yellow squash.

Yield: 4 servings.

Main Dish

Pistachio-Crusted Halibut with Dried Tomato Sauce and Black Bean Salsa

1	cup coconut milk	1	cup crushed saltines
1	egg	½	cup shelled pistachios
4	(6-ounce) halibut fillets, skin removed	2	tablespoons olive oil

Stir together coconut milk and egg in a shallow dish until blended; place fillets in mixture, and chill 30 minutes. Process saltines and pistachios in a food processor until coarsely ground. Dip fillets into saltine mixture until coated. Heat olive oil in a skillet until close to smoking; add fish, and cook 1 minute on each side. Remove from skillet, and place on a baking sheet; bake at 400° for approximately 12 minutes, depending on thickness. Place about 4 ounces Dried Tomato Sauce on serving plates; top with fillets, and spoon chilled salsa over top.

DRIED TOMATO SAUCE:

1	pint whipping cream	1	tablespoon fresh tarragon
1	cup dried tomatoes	2	ounces sherry

Bring cream to a boil in a heavy saucepan; boil until reduced by half. Remove from heat, and set aside. Place dried tomatoes in a pan with water to cover; let soak until soft, about 30 minutes. Drain and lightly rinse tomatoes. Process tomatoes, tarragon, and sherry in a food processor until mixture forms a smooth paste. Add paste to cream, and serve. This sauce cannot be reheated without breaking.

BLACK BEAN SALSA:

1	cup cooked, cooled black beans	1	teaspoon crushed red pepper
¼	cup diced purple onion	½	tablespoon sugar
¼	cup diced green bell pepper	3	tablespoons olive oil
¼	cup diced tomato	2	tablespoons red wine vinegar

Combine all ingredients; chill at least 1 hour before serving.

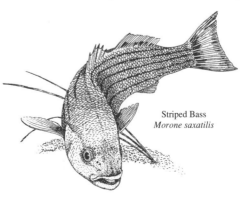

Striped Bass
Morone saxatilis

The "Canadian rule" for cooking fish states that a piece of fish should be cooked for 10 minutes per inch, measuring the fish at its thickest point. Cooking time can vary however, based on the type of fish, and thinner sections will cook faster, so check for doneness often during the cooking time.

Main Dish

Broiled Halibut in Mayonnaise Sauce

	Salt and pepper to taste
3½	pounds halibut fillets
½	cup mayonnaise (can substitute light but not nonfat)
1	tablespoon Worcestershire sauce
2	teaspoons lemon juice
1	tablespoon seafood seasoning

Sprinkle salt and pepper over fillets. Place fillets on greased rack of a broiler pan. Combine mayonnaise, Worcestershire, and lemon juice. Spread mixture over fillets. Sprinkle seafood seasoning on top. Broil 6 inches from heat (with electric oven door partially open) 20 minutes or until fish flakes easily with a fork.

Yield: 6 servings.

If fillets are very thick, bake at 350° until done.

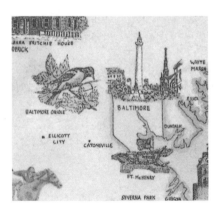

Main Dish

French Fish in a Packet

2 sheets aluminum foil (12 x 24 inches)

2 (5 to 6-ounce) firm fish fillets or steaks, or 1 (10-ounce) fillet, cut in half

1 small zucchini, thinly sliced

1 cup sliced mushrooms

½ purple onion, thinly sliced

2 tablespoons olive oil

Juice of 1 lemon

¼ cup dry white wine

Dash of salt and ground black pepper

1 tablespoon chopped fresh marjoram or basil or 1 teaspoon dried

6 ripe olives, halved

Fold each sheet of foil in half to form a double-thick square. Brush a little oil on center of each square. Rinse fish. On each square, layer half each of zucchini, mushrooms, fish, and onion slices. Combine olive oil, lemon juice, wine, salt and black pepper, and marjoram. Divide oil mixture, and pour over ingredients in each square, being careful not to spill. Forming the foil into open packets will help. Top with black olives, close packets. Bake at 400° for 20 minutes. Carefully avoiding the steam that will be released, open packets, and check that the fish is cooked. To serve, lift fish and vegetables with a spatula or large spoon onto individual serving dishes; pour liquid from packets over each serving.

Yield: 2 servings.

Striped Bass

Main Dish

Pappy's Southern Fried Catfish

Peanut Oil
5   pounds fresh catfish fillet
3   cups self-rising cornmeal
2   tablespoons self-rising flour
1   teaspoon salt
½   teaspoon pepper

Heat 2¾ inches peanut oil in a cast iron or heavy skillet until very hot, not boiling. Mix dry ingredients together and put into a brown paper bag or deep bowl. Drop catfish fillets into bag 3-4 pieces at a time. *Shake, rattle and roll* the bag vigorously to coat the fish well. Carefully drop the catfish fillets into the hot peanut oil to deep fry. Fry until catfish fillets float to the top. Then cook for another 1½ minutes, turning as necessary to brown evenly. Remove fish and place in a strainer or sieve to let oil drain from fillets. Place fish in a bowl lined with paper towels.

Catfish are chiefly freshwater fish with no scales. Though the skin is tough and needs to be removed before cooking, its firm flesh has a mild flavor and is low in fat. Late afternoons in the spring, there are many a fisherman preparing to catch a mess of catfish on trotlines. What is a trotline? An 80-foot fishing line with 30 fish hooks with about 30 inches between each hook. This line can be stretched across a river or lake by attaching to tree limbs, logs, or rocks. Lakes in warmer climates, such as those found in the South, may have cypress trees growing right out in the middle of the water. These evergreens have great root systems on which to tie a trotline. The fisherman will run or trot his line in the early evening and return the following morning for his catch. He may catch upwards of 50 pounds of fish on one line.

Main Dish

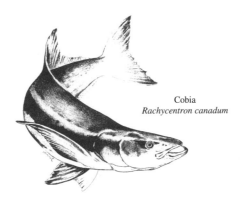

Cobia
Rachycentron canadum

Fresh Cobia with Mussel, Basil, Garlic, Tomato Sauce on Redneck Caviar

REDNECK CAVIAR:

2	cups stock (chicken, fish or vegetable)	1	teaspoon squid ink
1	cup stone ground grits		Dash salt
2	tablespoons whole butter		Dash pepper

COBIA:

4	6 ounce portions of cobia (½ inch thick or so)	½	chopped shallots
	Sea salt	16	mussels in shell
	Freshly ground black pepper	½	cup diced tomatoes
1	cup all purpose flour, on a plate for dredging	1	tablespoon chopped fresh basil
		2	teaspoons diced garlic
1	tablespoon clarified butter		Pinch of salt
½	cup dry white wine		Pinch of pepper
		1	tablespoon butter

Bring stock to a boil and add grits. Simmer for about 30 minutes. When grits reach the right consistency add butter and squid ink. Adjust salt and pepper to taste. Season both sides of the cobia fillets with salt and pepper. Dredge with flour. Shake off excess. Sauté cobia in cast iron pan with clarified butter until golden brown on both sides, 2-3 minutes. Simmer the shallots in white wine, add the mussels and cover to steam them open. Save the shallot, wine and mussel broth mixture. Pick the mussel meat out of the shell. Return the mussel meat back to the wine mixture and add the tomatoes, basil, garlic, pinch of salt and pepper. Simmer together for one minute. Add one tablespoon butter and swirl until butter is sauce. Put a dollop of Redneck Caviar in a bowl, then place a fillet of cobia on the caviar. Pour the shallot, mussel and wine mixture over the fillet.

Yield: 4 servings.

Main Dish

Wakefield Secret Shad Plank Sauce

1	(10 ounce) bottle of Lea & Perrin's Worcestershire sauce
1	pound lightly salted butter
12	lemons, juice only
2	tablespoons red cayenne pepper
4	tablespoons black pepper
½	cup salt

Place first 5 ingredients in a 2 to 3 quart stainless steel saucepan and bring to near boil. Add salt and remove from heat.

Yield: sauce for 2 large shad.

This recipe has been used as "The Sauce" for basting the shad at the Wakefield Ruritan Club's Inter-Community Shad Planking since 1948. This spring ritual is held, rain or shine, in Wakefield, Virginia on the third Wednesday in April. Our special thanks to the Nettles family for sharing their "Secret" recipe. This sauce is hot!

Reprinted from
The William & Mary Cookbook, © 1993

Bluegill
Lepomis macrochirus

Main Dish

Sautéed Shad Roe

2-3 sets of shad roe
6-8 slices bacon
¼-½ cup flour

2-4 tablespoons corn oil
1-2 lemons, sliced, for garnish

Separate shad roe sets, taking care not to tear membrane. Rinse; drain and dry well on paper toweling. Fry bacon and set aside; reserve bacon drippings in frying pan. Dredge each well-drained half of a shad roe set in flour; sauté in a mixture of hot bacon drippings and corn oil until roe is golden brown and cooked through. Depending on size of roe sets, the cooking usually takes 3-5 minutes per side. Drain well and serve with sliced lemons and slices of cooked bacon.

Yield: 2-4 servings.

Almost nothing will keep shad roe from popping.
It helps to keep the frying pan partially covered during cooking.
It also helps to remove pan from heat while you are turning the shad roe.

Reprinted from
The William & Mary Cookbook, © 1993

Sunrise Watermen

Main Dish

Fresh Shad Roe with Stone Ground Grits

3   large sets fresh shad roe
      Extra virgin olive oil
      Sea salt
      Freshly ground black pepper

BACON BUTTER:
¼   pound smoked bacon
4   ounces unsalted butter
1   ounce stock

GRITS:
1   cup stone ground grits
2   cups stock (chicken, fish or vegetable)
2   tablespoons whole butter
      Dash salt
      Dash pepper

Place the roe on an oven proof platter. Coat the roe well with olive oil and season both sides with salt and pepper. Place in a 350° oven and cook 5-6 minutes. Turn them over and cook another 3-4 minutes, keeping the center moist. Let rest in a warm place 10 minutes or so before serving. Chop the bacon into a small dice. Cook until near crispy in a heavy skillet and drain off excess fat. Cool the bacon, then put into a food processor with the butter and blend until smooth. Let the mixture cool. Cool the bacon butter and put it into a saucepan with half of the stock. Heat over medium heat, stirring constantly, until the butter has melted into a sauce-like consistency. Adjust the consistency with more stock (thinner) or butter (thicker). Cook the grits in the stock until creamy (30 minutes or so). Add cold butter and stir until dissolved. Adjust salt and pepper to taste. Place a generous spoon of grits in the center of a hot plate and arrange slices of roe around it. Spoon over some bacon sauce and garnish with parsley.

Yield: 6 servings.

Main Dish

Oven-Fried Fish

½ cup breadcrumbs
3 tablespoons grated Parmesan
   cheese
   Dash of salt

Dash of pepper
4-6 pieces firm fish fillets
1 beaten egg white

Combine first 4 ingredients. Dip fish into egg white, and coat with crumb mixture. Place fish on a baking sheet lined with aluminum foil and greased with vegetable cooking spray. Broil 6 inches from heat (with electric oven door partially open) 6 to 8 minutes, turning once. Fish may be cut into small pieces for serving.

Yield: 4 servings.

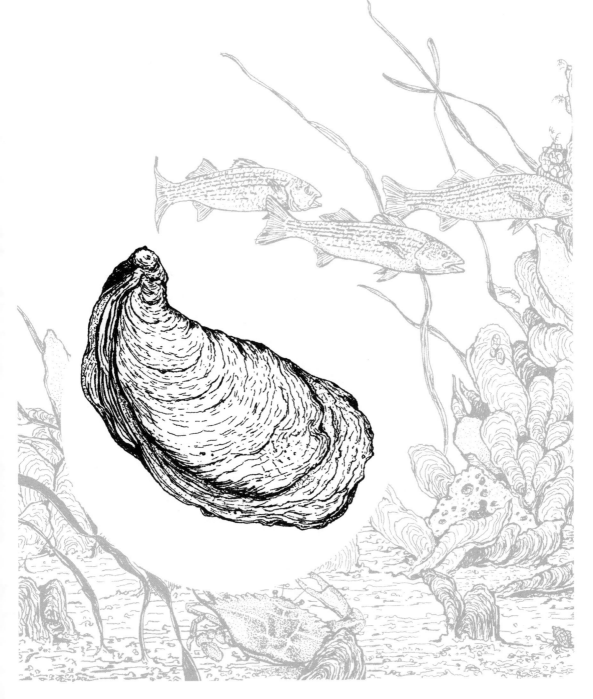

Oysters

OYSTERS

The Eastern oyster has played a major role not only in the fisheries of the Chesapeake, but in the ecology of the Bay as well. Oyster reefs or "rocks" were once the dominant feature of the Chesapeake Bay landscape. These reefs provide food and shelter for other organisms, and more importantly, serve as a living water filter. Oysters, like most bivalve mollusks, breathe and eat by pumping water over their gills. The gills absorb oxygen and strain out phytoplankton, the microscopic plants upon which oysters feed. Scientists estimate that the oyster population in the late 1800's would have been able to filter all the water in the Chesapeake Bay in only four or five days. It would take more than a year for the present oyster population to perform the same task. Because Chesapeake Bay oysters are no longer in great supply, wild and farmed oysters from the north and the Gulf are commonly found in Virginia seafood markets.

Oyster Dredge

Appetizer

Oyster Mousse

2	envelopes unflavored gelatin	2	tablespoons chopped fresh parsley
½	cup cold water		
1	(8-ounce) package cream cheese, softened	1	tablespoon Worcestershire sauce
1	cup mayonnaise	½	teaspoon garlic powder
2	(3.6-ounce) cans smoked oysters, drained and minced		Dash of hot sauce

Sprinkle gelatin over cold water, and set aside. Cook cream cheese and mayonnaise in a saucepan over low heat, stirring constantly, until cheese melts and mixture is smooth. Stir in next 5 ingredients and softened gelatin. Spoon into a well-greased 3½-cup mold. Cover and chill until set. Unmold and serve.

Yield: 24 servings.

***If desired, garnish with fresh parsley, lemon twists, and olives.
You may also halve the recipe for smaller quantity.***

Shucking Oysters

Soup/Stew

Is there truth to the saying that oysters should be eaten only during months with an "R" in their names? No. Oysters are safe and edible all year round, but during the summer months when they spawn, they are likely to be smaller than during the colder "R" months.

Autumn Spinach-and-Oyster Stew with Cornbread Croutons

1	tablespoon butter or margarine
8	ounces onions, peeled and finely chopped
4	ounces white leeks, peeled and finely chopped
4	ounces celery, peeled and finely chopped
6	ounces all-purpose flour
½	gallon fish stock
8	ounces white wine
	Several bay leaves
48	oysters (shuck, remove meat, save liquid)
8	ounces spinach
1	red bell pepper, cut into julienne strips
1	pint whipping cream
	Dash of salt
	Dash of pepper

Melt butter in a large saucepan over medium heat; add onion, leek, and celery; sauté until translucent. Dust vegetables with flour, and cook 5 to 7 minutes. Add fish stock; gradually add wine, and bring to a boil. Add bay leaves, and reduce heat. Simmer 30 minutes or until vegetables are tender. Pour through a wire-mesh strainer into a bowl. Puree vegetables in a food processor. Return vegetables and stock to saucepan over medium heat. Add oysters, spinach, and pepper strips. Temper with cream. Season to taste. Remove and discard bay leaves.

To serve, place oyster stew in bowl and top with cornbread croutons. To make the cornbread croutons, cut shapes out of previously made cornbread with decorative cookie cutters.

Yield: 1 gallon.

American Oyster
Crassostrea virginica

Soup/Stew

Green Chile-and-Oyster Chowder

1	pound red potatoes, cut into ½-inch cubes	½	cup fresh corn kernels
	Salted water	16	shucked oysters in their liquor
1	medium onion, finely chopped	1	large roasted pepper, peeled and cut into ½-inch pieces
2½	cups fish stock (or clam juice)	2	cups whipping cream
1	bay leaf		Dash of salt
½	pound fresh green chile peppers	1	tablespoon butter or margarine
2	cups peanut oil	1	teaspoon fresh marjoram, chopped

Bring potatoes and salted water (covered) to a boil in a large saucepan. Boil 4 minutes; cool. Cook onion, 1 cup stock, and bay leaf in a saucepan over low heat 15 to 20 minutes or until onion is tender but not browned. Discard bay leaf, and cool. Cook chiles in a skillet in hot peanut oil over medium heat 4 to 5 minutes or until skins are blistered. Cook corn in ¼ cup water in a covered saucepan 2 minutes or until tender. In a large saucepan, combine oysters with their liquor, remaining stock, and chiles. Heat 2 minutes; add potato, onion, and pepper, and bring to a boil. Add cream, keeping mixture below a boil to keep cream from separating. Add salt, corn, and butter. Pour into soup bowls, and garnish with fresh marjoram. Serve with cornbread, sliced tomato, and crab cakes, or as a wonderful main course for lunch.

Yield: 4 servings.

Oysters

The ingredients are precooked and added at the last minute so they retain flavor and identity. Use whole large oysters, as smaller ones dry out and don't have the plump, rich centers that are required. In this soup you do not want any hint of smokiness, so chiles are blistered in hot oil, not roasted or grilled.

Cook's Oyster House

Side Dish

Oyster Dressing

1	quart drained, chopped oysters
12	crumbled saltines
1	tablespoon rubbed sage
2	tablespoons butter or margarine, cut up
1	cup milk

Lightly grease a 7 x 12-inch baking dish with oil. Cover bottom of dish with half of oysters. Sprinkle with half of saltines. Sprinkle half of sage over crackers. Scatter half of butter over casserole. Repeat layers. Carefully pour milk along edges of dish. Bake at 450° for 45 minutes or until lightly browned.

Yield: 4 servings.

Side Dish

Scalloped Oysters

1	(12-ounce) container oysters, undrained
¼	cup sliced celery
2	tablespoons minced onion
2	tablespoons butter or margarine
1½	cups round buttery cracker crumbs
½	cup milk

1	tablespoon chopped fresh parsley
1	teaspoon lemon juice
½	teaspoon salt
¼	teaspoon garlic power
⅛	teaspoon freshly ground black pepper
½	cup (2 ounces) shredded Cheddar cheese

Pour oysters and liquid into a medium saucepan over medium-low heat. Simmer 5 minutes or until edges of oysters begin to curl. Drain, reserving 2 tablespoons liquid; set aside. Sauté celery and onion in butter until tender. Add cracker crumbs and next 6 ingredients, mixing well. Stir in oysters and reserved liquid. Spoon mixture into a lightly greased 1-quart baking dish. Bake, uncovered, at 375° degrees for 15 minutes. Sprinkle with cheese, and bake 5 more minutes or until cheese is bubbly. Garnish with additional chopped parsley.

Yield: 4 servings.

Dredging for Oysters

Main Dish

Chafing Dish Oysters, Ham, and Mushrooms

4	tablespoons butter or margarine
8	tablespoons all-purpose flour
1	cup milk
3	cups half-and-half
1	quart oysters, undrained
2	cups diced cured ham
1	pound mushrooms, sliced and sautéed in butter
	Dash of cayenne pepper
¼	cup dry white wine

Melt butter in a heavy 4-quart saucepan over medium heat; add flour, and stir until almost dry. Gradually add milk and cream; stir constantly until smooth and thickened. In a separate saucepan, simmer oysters and liquid over medium heat until edges curl. Add oysters, liquid, ham, and mushrooms to cream mixture. Gently stir to mix well. Pour into a chafing dish, light bottom of dish. Stir in cayenne pepper and wine. Serve over rice or English muffins. Great with a garden salad and a nice bottle of wine.

Yield: 8 servings.

Main Dish

Aussie Oyster Mornay Superb

2½ cups whole milk	1 teaspoon coarse-grained mustard
1 bunch green onions, chopped	
Dash of freshly ground pepper	1 tablespoon butter or margarine
Dash of salt	1 large carrot, finely scraped and grated
5 drops hot sauce	
Pinch of dried basil or dill	½ cup whole cream
½ pinch celery salt	24 oysters in the shell
2 tablespoons all-purpose flour	Shredded cheese

Combine first 7 ingredients in a large saucepan over medium heat. Combine flour and mustard and enough water to form a smooth paste. When milk mixture is very hot, but not boiling, stir in flour mixture. Add butter, and stir until thickened. Reduce heat to low, and cook, stirring occasionally, 13 minutes. Be careful not to let it burn or stick. Stir in grated carrot. Remove from heat, and stir in cream. Remove oysters from their shells, and add to sauce in saucepan. Return pan to stove to heat thoroughly. Heat shells under a hot grill. When all is ready, fill shells with oysters and sauce. Sprinkle with shredded cheese, and place under grill to brown. Serve with salad, grilled fish, baked potatoes, and sherbet.

Yield: 2 to 4 servings.

Tonging for Oysters

Oysters can be opened in the microwave. Clean them, and place them in a glass dish. Microwave on the "defrost" setting for 1 to 2 minutes. To open and cook the meat at the same time, microwave for 2 to 3 minutes on the "high" setting.

Main Dish

Oyster Loaf

12	large oysters
	Dash of salt
	Dash of ground white pepper
	All-purpose flour or pancake mix
	Vegetable oil
1	loaf French bread
½	cup butter or margarine
3	garlic cloves, crushed
1	tablespoon chopped fresh parsley
8	slices bacon, cooked and drained
8	slices fresh tomato, seared
	Mayonnaise
	Prepared horseradish

Drain and pat oysters dry. Season oysters with salt and white pepper; roll oysters in flour or pancake mix. (If oysters are unwashed, salt may not be needed.) Pour enough oil into a skillet to completely cover oysters. Heat oil; fry oysters to golden brown. Drain on paper towels. Cut bread loaf in half horizontally; hollow out both halves. Melt butter in a small saucepan; sauté garlic and parsley in butter until tender. Brush bread halves with butter and garlic mixture. Place bacon in bottom half of bread. Top bacon with fried oysters and tomato slices. Place top half of bread loaf on top of tomatoes; wrap loaf in aluminum foil. Bake at 350° for 10 minutes. Remove from oven, slice, and serve hot with mayonnaise and/or horseradish. Tartar sauce, shredded lettuce, ketchup, hot sauce, and lemon wedges are also good with this dish. Doesn't freeze well, as there are never any leftovers to freeze!

Yield: 2 servings.

Main Dish

Claibo's Eggplant and Oysters

1	medium eggplant, peeled and cubed	½	cup dry breadcrumbs
¼	cup butter or margarine	1	pint oysters, undrained
4	tablespoons chopped onion	½	cup light cream
			Salt and pepper to taste

Bring eggplant to a boil in small amount of lightly salted water until tender. Drain eggplant. Melt butter in a separate saucepan; sauté onion in butter until tender. Add half of breadcrumbs to onion mixture. In a third saucepan, heat oysters in their liquid over medium heat until they curl. Drain oysters. Combine eggplant, onion mixture, oysters, and cream; season with salt and pepper to taste. Place mixture in a lightly greased baking dish. Cover with remaining breadcrumbs. Bake at 350° for 25-30 minutes (until breadcrumbs are brown).

Yield: 6 servings.

The Samuel H. Hermon Oyster Boat

Main Dish

Oysters Mosca

½ cup butter or margarine
1 large onion, chopped
3 garlic cloves, minced
2 tablespoons chopped fresh parsley
½ teaspoon dried thyme
¾ teaspoon dried oregano
⅛ teaspoon ground red pepper
   Dash of salt
   Dash of pepper
4 dozen oysters, drained (reserve liquid)
1 cup Italian-seasoned breadcrumbs
2 slices bacon, fried and crumbled
10 almonds, crushed
   Grated Parmesan cheese

Melt butter in a saucepan over medium heat; sauté onion in butter until clear. Add garlic and next 7 ingredients. Cook until oysters curl at edges; add reserved liquid from oysters. Fold in breadcrumbs, bacon, and almonds. Spoon into a greased baking dish. Top with Parmesan cheese. Bake at 350° for 15 to 20 minutes. This recipe is the most representative yet for an oyster dish served at Mosca's Restaurant in Waggaman, LA, just outside of New Orleans. A plain, white-sided building, Mosca's exterior resembles a south Louisiana honkytonk and hides an incredibly talented kitchen known for its Italian dishes with Cajun flavor. The 20-minute drive across the Huey P. Long Bridge is well worth it.

Yield: 4 servings.

Main Dish

Deviled Oysters

1-2 teaspoons butter or margarine, melted	1 tablespoon fresh lemon juice
1 pint select oysters, drained (reserve oyster liquor)	1 tablespoon Worcestershire sauce
¼ teaspoon salt	3 tablespoons light cream
⅛ teaspoon freshly ground black pepper	1 tablespoon freshly minced parsley
2 tablespoons horseradish	⅛ teaspoon sweet Hungarian paprika

TOPPING:

¼ cup butter or margarine, melted	⅓ cup fine bread crumbs

Preheat oven to 375°. Lightly brush 6 individual seafood baking dishes with melted butter or margarine; divide oysters among the dishes. Sprinkle with salt and pepper. Combine ¼ cup reserve oyster liquor with horseradish and next 4 ingredients; spoon over oysters. Mix topping ingredients and spoon over oysters. Bake for 20 minutes or until golden brown. Serve hot!

Yield: 6 servings.

*An old-fashioned oyster dish
that's guaranteed to please!*

*Reprinted from
The William & Mary Cookbook, © 1993*

For alumni of the '30s and '40s, some of their most treasured college memories focus on the Travis House. Many worked as costumed waiters, and others had the pleasure of dining in the candlelit rooms of Williamsburg's first colonial restaurant.

Main Dish

Travis House Escalloped Oysters

½   cup butter or margarine
½   cup flour
1½ teaspoons paprika
½   teaspoon salt
¼   teaspoon black pepper
     Dash cayenne
1   onion, finely chopped
½   green pepper, finely chopped
½   bud garlic, finely minced
1   teaspoon lemon juice
1   tablespoon Worcestershire sauce
1   quart oysters, heated in their own liquor
¼   cup cracker crumbs

Melt butter or margarine, add flour and cook for 5 minutes or until light brown. Stir constantly. Add paprika, salt, black pepper and cayenne. Cook for 3 minutes. Add onion and green pepper. Add garlic and cook slowly for 5 minutes. Take from the fire and add lemon juice, Worcestershire sauce and oysters. Pour into a baking dish, sprinkle cracker crumbs over the top. Bake in oven at 400° for 30 minutes.

Reprinted from
The William & Mary Cookbook, © 1993

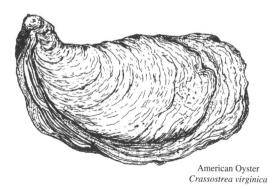

American Oyster
Crassostrea virginica

The following account from a member of the class of 1943 records the Travis House at its height of popularity: "The Travis House was my favorite restaurant during the years that I lived in Williamsburg. In addition to a gracious ambiance, the food was superb and artfully served. Early arrivals were ushered upstairs to a charmingly appointed drawing room with a fireplace, always glowing in winter. Waiting for a table was a most pleasant and romantic interlude as attentive waiters served claret or champagne. Even on busy evenings, one never felt rushed. Travis House dinners remain a wonderful memory."

The Travis House, one of the original eighteenth-century Williamsburg houses, was built on Francis Street in 1765. In 1929 it was moved to the Duke of Gloucester Street, midway between the Capitol and the College. In 1930 it opened as an ordinary serving traditional colonial food. For the next twenty-one years, guests at the Travis House enjoyed dinner at noon and in the evening, or tea in the afternoon. In fair weather, guests were delighted to find meals served in the garden. Afternoon tea was served in boxwood-enclosed garden rooms or in one of two garden tea houses.

In 1951 the Travis house was closed as a restaurant and was returned to the southwest corner of Francis and Henry streets. In 1968 the Travis house was once again relocated - this time to its original eighteenth-century location on the northwest corner of Francis and Henry streets. Based on the memories of the classes of the '30s and '40s, many alumni will view the Travis House with a new perspective after tasting these Escalloped Oysters!

Main Dish

Colonial Oysters and Ham

6	frozen patty shells
1	teaspoon instant chicken bouillon
$\frac{1}{2}$	cup warm water
1	pint oysters, standard or select
3	tablespoons butter
3	tablespoons flour
$\frac{1}{2}$	cup oyster liquor
1	cup whipping cream, unwhipped
$\frac{1}{8}$	teaspoon dry mustard
$\frac{1}{2}$	teaspoon lemon juice
$\frac{1}{4}$	teaspoon Worcestershire sauce
$\frac{1}{8}$	teaspoon onion salt
2	tablespoons butter
$\frac{2}{3}$	cup diced cooked country or Smithfield ham

TOPPING:

$\frac{1}{8}$	teaspoon freshly cracked pepper
1-2	teaspoons chopped fresh parsley

Bake patty shells by directions on package; cool. Dissolve bouillon in warm water and set aside. Drain oysters and reserve liquor. Melt butter over low heat; stir in flour and allow to bubble for 1 minute. Do not brown. Remove from heat and slowly stir in bouillon, oyster liquor and cream. Return to low heat and stir until thickened. Add mustard, lemon juice, Worcestershire sauce and onion salt. Remove from heat, cover and set aside. Sauté oysters in butter only until edges curl and oysters are just firm. Drain. Stir in oysters and ham into sauce and heat gently over low heat. Spoon into patty shells and top with cracked pepper and chopped parsley. Serve immediately.

Yield: 6 servings.

Has been popular for generations!

Reprinted from
The William & Mary Cookbook, © 1993

Clams
Scallops
Mussels

CLAMS, SCALLOPS, MUSSELS

CLAMS

The hard clam, also known as the hardshell clam or quahog, is the clam most often served in the Chesapeake Bay area. This mollusk has been a source of food for humans for centuries, as evidenced by ancient piles of shell, called middens, which can be found in the Chesapeake Bay area. The thick shell's interior has streaks of brilliant purple on white, which inspired its use by native Americans for making beads. These bead necklaces were used as money or "wampum. "

Clams are marketed in the shell, fresh shucked, canned or frozen. Fresh unshucked hard clams should have tightly closed shells; discard any clam with a gaping shell which will not remain closed. Do not keep live clams in water or in an air-tight container or they will die from lack of oxygen. Wrap them in damp paper towels, store in the refrigerator, and use them within 2 -3 days. The term "cherrystone" indicates the size, not the species, of clam. Hard clams are marketed as "chowders," "cherrystones," "topnecks" and "littlenecks. " These market terms refer to the size of the clam, with chowders the largest and littlenecks the smallest. The smaller clams are more tender and more expensive. Hard clams have become a major aquaculture product in Virginia and are marketed all over the United States and exported to other countries.

SCALLOPS

Scallops are the source of the beautiful fan-shaped shell which has been used as a decorative design, as a religious symbol and even as a commercial trademark. This shellfish is also highly prized for its sweet meat. Most Americans have eaten only the scallop's round, marshmallow-shaped adductor muscle, which is the part of the scallop commonly marketed in the United States. This muscle is shucked from the shell, and the rest of the scallop is discarded. However, like clams and oysters, the entire soft body of the scallop is edible. In Europe, scallops are commonly served raw and whole on the half shell.

The sea scallop is the largest of the scallops and also supports the largest commercial scallop fishery. Its large adductor muscle provides the strength needed for the scallop to swim by clapping together the two halves of its shell. The bay scallop is smaller than the sea scallop, but its taste is sweeter. Bay scallops were once common in the Chesapeake, but their numbers have dwindled along with the seagrass beds which provide their habitat. Successful aquaculture of bay scallops has helped bring back the market supply.

Scallops are unable to close their shell tightly, so they quickly dry out and die once they are removed from the water. For this reason, they are usually shucked at sea as soon as they are caught. Fresh scallops should have a sweet, ocean smell.

Look for firm meat with a creamy white or slight pink color. Occasionally scallop meats will have an orange or pink discoloration caused by the leaching of the color from the roe into the meat. This does not affect the quality or flavor of the scallop.

Don't overcook scallops! Stop cooking when the outside of the meat becomes opaque. The inside of the scallop will still be a bit translucent, but it is perfectly safe to eat and will be much tastier than a scallop cooked through until it's dry.

MUSSELS

Mussels are unique among their bivalve relatives due to their "beard," a tough cluster of threads which anchor the mussels to rocks, other shells or plants. The blue mussel is the most common edible mussel in the Eastern United States. The shells of blue mussels range in color from bluish-black to brown, and the meat can also vary in color from whitish to orange. To clean mussels, remove the beard and wash well. Discard any mussel that remains open when tapped. Steam the mussels in white wine with a little garlic and fresh herbs until the shells open.

Clams

Appetizer

Hot Clam Dip

1	cup chopped onion
2	garlic cloves, chopped
½	cup butter or margarine
2	(10-ounce) cans minced clams with juice
1½	cups seasoned breadcrumbs
1	tablespoon dried oregano
2	tablespoons chopped fresh parsley
2	tablespoons fresh lemon juice
	Dash of hot sauce
⅓	cup grated Parmesan cheese

Sauté onion and garlic in butter until tender. Combine clams and next 5 ingredients in a medium bowl; stir in onion mixture. Place dip in a large pie plate, and sprinkle with cheese. Bake at 350° for 40 minutes or until bubbly and browned. Serve with crackers.

Basket of Clams

Appetizer

Clams Baked with Fresh Basil, Dried Tomatoes and Roasted Garlic

4	dozen Cherrystone clams, washed thoroughly	4	garlic cloves, sliced very thin, browned over medium heat, dried on paper towels
2	tablespoons finely diced yellow onion	4	tablespoons grated Parmesan cheese
2	tablespoons olive oil	¼	teaspoon ground cumin
6	tablespoons fresh basil, chopped	4	tablespoons breadcrumbs
¾	cup dried tomatoes, chopped		Dash of salt
			Dash of pepper

Open clams, detach clam from shells, and place each on 1 half shell. Sauté onion in hot oil over medium heat until translucent. Add basil, tomato, and garlic. Cook, stirring constantly, 1 to 2 minutes; turn contents of pan into a bowl. Stir in Parmesan cheese, cumin, and breadcrumbs. Season to taste with salt and pepper. Cover each clam with ½ teaspoon mixture; chill until ready to bake. Bake at 400° until clams are hot.

Yield: 4 servings.

Hardshell Clam
Mercenaria mercenaria

Soup/Stew

Finest Kind of Clam Chowder

¼	pound bacon
1	quart diced potato
1	large onion, chopped
1	quart Maine clams, undrained
1	quart milk, scalded
	Dash of pepper
	Dash of salt
1	tablespoon butter or margarine

Dice bacon; fry in a large stockpot until brown. Add potato and onion with just enough water to cover potato. Cook over low heat, just simmering, until tender. Drain clams, reserving juice. Add clams to potato mixture; bring to a boil. Boil 2 minutes. (Any longer will make clams tough.) Remove from heat, and let stand a few minutes. Add hot milk and reserved clam juice, and season to taste. Add butter just before serving. For best flavor, chill chowder at least 3 to 4 hours. Aging is as important for clam chowder as for lobster stew. If you can wait until the next day it will be that much finer. Have lots of heated crackers ready. Freezes well.

Yield: 6 to 8 servings.

Soup/Stew

Sea Scallop, Fresh Corn, and Tomato Chowder

1½ pounds sea scallops
1 large yellow onion, finely chopped
2 ancho peppers, seeded and thinly sliced
1 green bell pepper, seeded and diced
1 red bell pepper, seeded and diced
¼ cup canola oil
4 stalks celery, finely chopped
3 carrots, finely chopped
2 garlic cloves, chopped
½ cup all-purpose flour
2 quarts water
Whole corn kernels from 8 ears fresh corn
6 large tomatoes, seeded and chopped
4 potatoes, scrubbed well and diced
½ teaspoon ground cumin
1 bunch parsley, washed, stems removed, and leaves chopped
¼ cup sherry
2 cups whipping cream
Corn tortillas
Vegetable oil

Prepare scallops by removing and discarding side mussels; chill scallops. Sauté onion, ancho peppers, and bell peppers in hot oil in a large saucepan over high heat until vegetables are tender and partly seared. Reduce heat to medium; add celery, carrots, and garlic. Sauté until tender; remove from heat, and stir in flour. Add 2 quarts water and next 6 ingredients. Bring to a boil; reduce heat, and simmer until potato is cooked. Add cream and scallops; simmer until scallops are just cooked. Cut tortillas into strips. In a separate skillet, heat oil to 350°; fry tortilla strips until crisp. Remove to paper towels. Serve soup hot, sprinkled with tortilla strips.

Yield: 4 servings.

RICHMOND

Salad

Warm Scallop Salad

	Juice from 2 lemons
3	tablespoons extra virgin olive oil
1/3	teaspoon celery seed
	Dash of salt
	Dash of white pepper
2-3	Belgian endive, cut into julienne strips (size of blades of grass)
1	cup all-purpose flour
1	teaspoon salt
1/2	teaspoon cayenne pepper
1/2	teaspoon dried oregano
1	egg
1/2	cup milk
2	large shallots, finely sliced into rings
2	sweet onions, finely sliced into rings
2	cups vegetable oil
8-12	large sea scallops, rinsed
1/2	teaspoon seafood seasoning
1/8	teaspoon kosher salt

Bay Scallop
Argopecten irradians

Whisk together first 3 ingredients in a medium bowl. Add salt and white pepper to taste. Add endive strips, tossing well; chill mixture. Combine flour and next 3 ingredients in a nonmetal bowl. In a separate bowl, whisk together egg and milk until blended. Combine shallots and sweet onions in egg mixture. Reserve 2 tablespoons vegetable oil, and heat remaining oil in a medium sauté pan. Remove onions to flour mixture, and coat one-fourth at a time. Place onions in hot oil, arranging each batch into the shape of a small bird's nest. Cook each nest, turning once, until golden brown. Remove nests to paper towels to drain. Combine reserved oil, seafood seasoning, and kosher salt in a nonmetal bowl. Add scallops, stirring to coat. Arrange endive mixture at center of 4 serving plates. Place an onion nest on each plate. Drizzle any remaining dressing around

(Continued on next page)

(Warm Scallop Salad, continued)

each plate. Heat a nonstick skillet over medium heat. Cook scallops about 5 minutes, turning once. Remove to the center of each nested salad plate; serve immediately.

Yield: 4 servings.

Scallop

Main Dish

Scallop Stir-Fry

2	garlic cloves
1/4	cup lite soy sauce
1	pound scallops, cut into bite-size pieces and drained
2-3	tablespoons vegetable oil
1/2	cup carrots, cut in 1/2-inch pieces
1/2	cup chopped onion
1	large yellow or red bell pepper, cut into strips
3/4	cup broccoli florets, cut into bite-size pieces
1	stalk celery, sliced crosswise in 1-inch pieces

Crush 1 garlic clove, and add to soy sauce; pour mixture over scallops. Heat oil in frying pan or wok. Thinly slice remaining garlic clove, and stir-fry until browned. Remove garlic from pan. Stir-fry carrots until crisp-tender; add onion, bell pepper, broccoli and celery. Stir-fry until vegetables are crisp-tender. Remove vegetables to another container. Drain scallops, reserving marinade. Stir-fry scallops until translucent; return vegetables to pan, and add marinade. Cook until thoroughly heated. Serve over rice with tossed salad.

Yield: 4 servings.

Main Dish

Steamed Sea Scallops and Country Ham

¾	pound large, fresh sea scallops
2	tablespoons medium dry sherry
1	(1-inch) piece ginger, grated
⅓	cup chopped scallions, including green part
⅓	cup sliced fresh mushrooms
⅓	cup shaved or thinly sliced country ham
⅓	cup whipping cream
4	servings fettuccine, cooked al dente

Marinate scallops in sherry 15 minutes; drain. Place layers of marinated scallops, ginger, scallions, mushrooms, and ham (in that order) in a steamer above ¾ cup water; steam 5 to 7 minutes. Remove steamer tray, and keep contents warm. Reduce the liquid remaining in steamer base to ⅓ cup at a hard boil. Add cream; return just to a boil, and remove from heat. Serve scallop mixture (keeping layers intact during serving) together with cream sauce over fettuccine.

Yield: 4 servings.

**If scallops are very large,
slice them horizontally in half.**

Virginia Institute of Marine Science
Gloucester Point, VA
Clamming

Mussels

Main Dish

Mussels Marinara

2	pounds mussels in shells, scrubbed and debearded	1	(14½-ounce) can stewed tomatoes, drained and chopped
1	tablespoon olive oil	2	bay leaves
1	medium onion, diced, or 2 tablespoons instant minced onion	1	tablespoon dried basil
		2	tablespoons dried parsley flakes
2	teaspoons dry garlic chips	⅛	teaspoon coarsely ground black pepper
		½	cup white wine

Wash the mussels in cold water; drain in a colander. Discard any that remain open. A healthy mussel will close its shell when washed. Discard beards, hairy appendages outside the shell. When transporting mussels, keep them in shaved ice. Simmer oil and next 8 ingredients in a large stockpot 5 minutes. Add mussels; cover and steam 5 to 8 minutes, shaking the pan every 1 to 2 minutes. Serve over hot linguine. When serving mussels, furnish a waste bowl for the shells.

Use a mixture of mussels and clams in shells. Omit linguine, and serve in deep soup bowls as a first course. You may also omit mussels and substitute 1 pound raw peeled shrimp or 1 pound small bay scallops. In this variation, use a large skillet; add shrimp or scallops after initial 5 minutes of cooking. Simmer until seafood is no longer translucent (5 to 10 minutes). This recipe is then called **Shrimp** *or* **Scallops à la Provençale** *and serves 4 people. You may also use a mixture of scallops, shrimp, and mussels. For a Portuguese character, use a mixture of shrimp, mussels, diced cooked pork, and 1 can baby clams, drained. Serve over rice instead of linguine. For plain steamed mussels as a first course or as a main dish over linguine, omit stewed tomatoes and substitute ¼ cup butter or margarine for olive oil. Increase wine to 1 cup, and add 1 teaspoon dried thyme. All variations may be easily adapted to outdoor cooking on a grill, in a pit, or on camp stove, on which you can use a small kettle or frying pan.*

Yield: 2 servings.

**The French, Belgians, and Germans usually opt to drink beer
with mussels. This is a low fat/heart-healthy meal.**

VIMS Scientist Mike Oesterling with Tray of Scallops

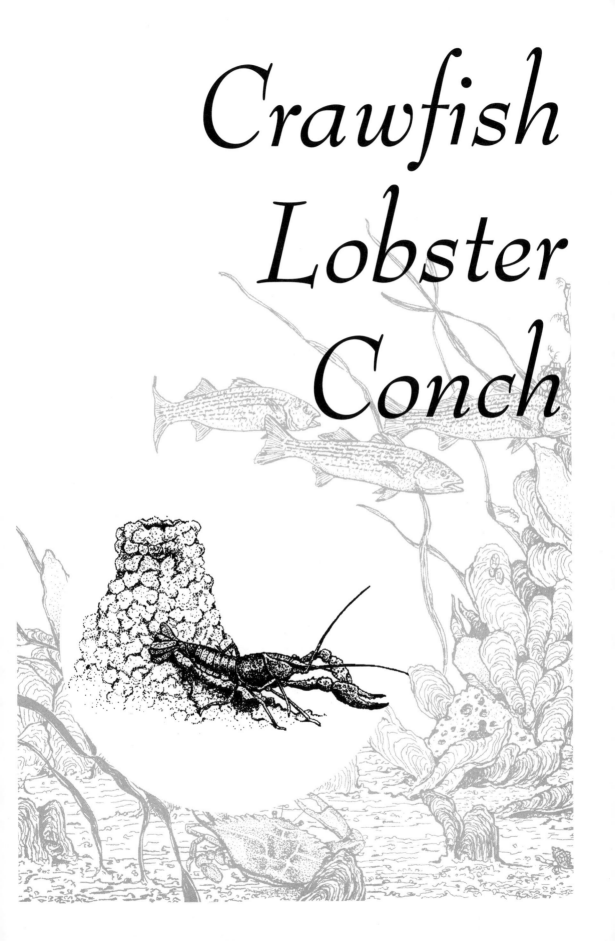

Crawfish
Lobster
Conch

CRAWFISH, LOBSTER, CONCH

CRAWFISH

Crawfish, crayfish, crawdads, or mudbugs—all these names refer to the same freshwater crustacean which resembles a little lobster. Long a signature seafood in Cajun and Creole cuisine, the crawfish is now popular nationwide. Due to the success of crawfish aquaculture, these crustaceans are available in many restaurants and seafood markets. They may be purchased live, whole frozen and as frozen tail meat. Five to six pounds of whole crawfish will yield one pound of meat.

To cook live crawfish, fill a large pot with enough water to cover them. Add salt, crab boil, lemon, garlic, or other seasonings. Bring water to a full boil and then add the live crawfish. Cover, turn off heat and let sit for about ten minutes.

To eat a whole crawfish, twist the tail portion away from the rest of the body. Peel the shell away from the tailmeat, similar to peeling a shrimp. For a real Cajun treat, suck out the flavorful juices from the head portion.

LOBSTER

The American lobster ranges from Virginia to Labrador, but it is in the cold waters north of Cape Cod that lobsters are most common. They are unmistakable among the crustaceans due to their large size, sometimes over 40 pounds. Their large front claws are asymmetrical, one pointed and sharp for grasping and tearing, the other stout and rounded for crushing.

The sweet tail and claw meat of lobsters is highly prized by seafood lovers. When purchasing a live lobster, choose one which moves its legs and curls its tail under its body when picked up. Never purchase a dead lobster. Like crabmeat, lobster meat is delicate and prone to rapid decomposition. A 1 to 2 pound lobster is cooked by boiling it in water for about 5 minutes then simmering for 15 to 20 minutes. Lobster is also available as frozen lobster tails and picked meat.

WHELKS AND CONCHS

Whelk and conch shells are familiar beach souvenirs, held to the ear to recall the sound of the ocean. The tough, yellowish egg strings of the whelk are often found washed up on mid-Atlantic beaches after a storm. These strings are made of a series of round, flat capsules, each one containing numerous tiny whelk eggs.

Whelks are not common on seafood menus in most of the United States. However, they are very popular in many large Northern cities and in some mid-

Atlantic coastal localities, where they may appear as "conch chowder." Whelks are commonly called conchs, but true conchs are found in warmer waters in the south Atlantic and the Caribbean. Conch is a popular food item in the Florida Keys and the Caribbean. Knobbed and channeled whelks are the two species commercially harvested in Virginia. The meat is removed from the shell by steaming or by mechanically crushing the shell. The edible portion is the large fleshy "foot." It is chopped or sliced and can be fried or used in soups, chowders and salads.

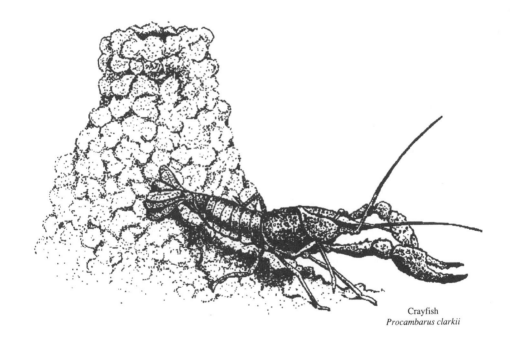

Crayfish
Procambarus clarkii

Soup/Stew

Bahamian Conch Chowder

1	quart conch, diced
4	ounces bacon or pork slices
2	onions, diced
6	large potatoes, diced
4	tomatoes, sliced
2	teaspoons salt
¼	teaspoon pepper

Wash and drain conch. Cook bacon and onion in a skillet over medium heat until onion is lightly browned. Add potato and tomato; add water to cover. Add salt and pepper, and cook slowly 30 minutes. Add conch, and cook slowly 10 to 15 minutes.

Yield: 6 servings.

Clams can be substituted for conch. Sherry or peppers can be added to increase the flavor. Bacon can be omitted to reduce fat.

Preparing Seafood in Sea Grant Test Kitchen

Casserole

Lobster Casserole

1	cup butter or margarine
1	cup chopped celery
½	pound fresh mushrooms, sliced
½	medium onion, chopped
1	green bell pepper, chopped
3	cups water
½	teaspoon salt
1	(2-ounce) jar diced pimiento
2	(10¾-ounce) cans cream of mushroom soup
½	cup milk
2	(12- to 16-ounce) cans lobster meat
1	cup wild rice, cooked
½	cup slivered almonds

Melt butter in a skillet over medium heat; sauté celery, mushrooms, onion, and bell pepper 6 minutes or until tender. Stir in remaining ingredients, except almonds; pour into a baking dish. Top with almonds. Bake at 350° for 40 to 45 minutes. Serve over patty shells. This dish may be made a day in advance. Wait to top with almonds until ready to cook.

Spiny Lobster

Main Dish

Lobster Newburg

1	**(2-pound) lobster**
¼	**cup butter or margarine**
½	**teaspoon paprika**
½	**cup sherry**
4	**tablespoons all-purpose flour**
1½	**cups thin cream**
2	**egg yolks, beaten**
½	**cup (2 ounces) shredded Cheddar cheese (mild or sharp)**
¾	**cup sautéed mushrooms**
4	**slices white bread**

Steam whole lobster for 2 minutes. Remove meat, and cut into small pieces. Melt butter in a double boiler. Stir in paprika, sherry, and lobster meat. Sprinkle with flour, and fold into mixture. Add cream and egg yolks to double boiler; blend until mixture thickens. Add cheese and mushrooms and cook until cheese dissolves. Remove crusts from bread, and fit bread neatly in muffin tins. Bake at 300° for 15 minutes. Pour lobster mixture into baked bread cups. Serve with a nice white wine and dinner salad.

Yield: 4 servings.

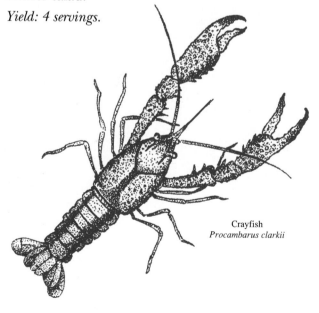

Crayfish
Procambarus clarkii

Main Dish

Crawfish Étouffée

½	cup butter or margarine
1	large onion, chopped
2	stalks celery, chopped
½	green bell pepper, chopped
1	teaspoon sugar
¼	cup tomato paste
1	tablespoon paprika (or 1 teaspoon cayenne pepper)
½	teaspoon salt
1	teaspoon ground black pepper
	Dash of thyme
1	bay leaf
1	tablespoon cornstarch
1	cup chicken broth or ½ cup white wine plus ½ cup water
1	pound boiled, peeled crawfish tails (or shrimp)
1	tablespoon green onion tops, cut with scissors
½	teaspoon Kitchen Bouquet seasoning

Melt butter in a large heavy saucepan. (Do not use a cast-iron skillet, as it will discolor the crawfish.) Sauté onion, celery, and bell pepper in butter until tender. Stir in sugar, tomato paste, paprika, salt, black pepper, thyme, and bay leaf. Simmer, stirring occasionally, 20 minutes. In a separate container, dissolve cornstarch in broth; add to pot. Cook for 20 minutes or until sauce thickens. Add crawfish, half a tablespoon green onion and Kitchen Bouquet. Serve over steamed or boiled rice topped with green onion slices. This dish is even better when chilled overnight!

Yield: 4 servings.

Crayfish

Seafood Combinations

Soup/Stew

Shrimp
Penaeus spp.

Seafood Gumbo

⅔	cup vegetable oil or bacon drippings
1	cup all-purpose flour
3	large onions, chopped
3	stalks celery, chopped
5-6	garlic cloves, chopped
¼	large green bell pepper, chopped
2	quarts water
3	bay leaves
	Dash of hot sauce
	Dash of pepper
	Dash of salt
	Worcestershire sauce
2-3	pounds okra, washed and sliced
2	(8-ounce) cans tomato sauce
1	dozen crabs, cleaned
1	bunch green onions, chopped
1	small bunch parsley, chopped
3	pounds shrimp, peeled and deveined
2	pounds crabmeat, bits of shell removed
1	pint oysters

Make a roux by stirring oil and flour in a skillet over medium heat until chocolate brown in color. Add chopped vegetables, and sauté until tender. Transfer to large gumbo pot (not cast-iron, as iron will make okra turn black). Add water, and bring to a boil. Add seasonings, okra, and tomato sauce. Boil for 1 hour. Add crabs, green onions, and parsley. Boil 20 minutes, adding shrimp 2 to 3 minutes after crabs. Just before serving, add crabmeat and oysters. Serve over hot fluffy rice in gumbo bowls.

Omit okra or tomato sauce. Instead of seafood, use a large hen, wild duck, geese, turkey carcass, or any other type of meat. Cook until tender.

Yield: 12 servings.

Soup/Stew

Fish Chowder

2	tablespoons butter or margarine			Dash of salt
1	pound scrod, deboned			Dash of pepper
½	pound shrimp		1	(10¾-ounce) can cream of shrimp soup
½	pound scallops		1	can Cheddar cheese soup
2	cups milk		2	tablespoons sherry
	Chopped parsley			

Melt butter in a double boiler. Add scrod, shrimp, scallops, 1 cup milk, parsley, salt and pepper. Simmer, stirring often, over medium heat 25 minutes or until all fish is cooked. Add both soups and remaining milk; simmer until well blended. Add sherry just before serving. Serve warm with oyster crackers.

Yield: 8 servings.

Crab Feast

Soup/Stew

Italian Fish Soup

3	leeks, cleaned and sliced (white part only)
2	garlic cloves, minced
1	yellow onion, peeled and chopped
1	cup chopped celery
1	cup sliced fresh mushrooms
½	cup olive oil
6	cups fish stock, clam juice, or water
1	cup tomato sauce
1	cup dry white wine
	Dash of salt
	Dash of cayenne pepper
2	pounds shellfish (combination crab, unpeeled shrimp, clams, and mussels)
1	pound boneless white fish fillet, sea bass, or cod, cut into small pieces
2	tablespoons chopped fresh parsley

Sauté leeks, garlic, onion, celery, and mushrooms in hot oil in a large heavy stockpot until onion is translucent. Add stock, tomato sauce, and white wine; and simmer. Add salt and cayenne pepper to taste. Add shellfish, clams and mussels first, as they take longer to cook. Simmer until fish is tender. Garnish with parsley. Serve with mixed green salad and buttermilk-jalapeño cornbread.

Yield: 8 servings.

Because fish is high in protein and low in cholesterol, it makes a healthy and delicious substitute for red meat. Try fish in place of beef in tacos and pasta dishes.

Soup/Stew

Winter Seafood Gumbo

1	medium onion, chopped	1	garlic clove, minced
1	green bell pepper, chopped	4	cups chicken broth (defatted)
1	tablespoon olive oil	1	can tomatoes, chopped
1	bay leaf	2	cups frozen okra
½	teaspoon each dried parsley flakes, dried thyme, celery seed	1	cup canned crabmeat, bits of shell removed
¼	teaspoon salt and pepper	1	cup canned shrimp
2	dashes of hot sauce	1	cup uncooked rice

Sauté onion and bell pepper in hot oil in a Dutch oven. Add next 8 ingredients, and simmer, stirring occasionally, 1 hour or until okra breaks up. Add seafood during last 5 minutes. In a separate saucepan, cook rice in 2 cups water 20 minutes or until done; set aside. Add crabmeat and shrimp. Cook until thoroughly heated. Ladle into bowls, and place a large spoonful of rice in the middle.

Yield: 4 servings.

Fresh crabmeat and shrimp may also be used.

Salad

Seafood Caesar Salad

6	ounces olive oil
2	teaspoons Dijon mustard
1	egg yolk
2	anchovies, well mashed
2	garlic cloves, well mashed
2	shallots, finely chopped
2	heads romaine lettuce, washed, drained, and torn into bite-size pieces
1	pound poached salmon fillet, flaked into large chunks
1	pound steamed shrimp, peeled, deveined, cut in half
½	pound lump crabmeat, bits of shell removed Freshly grated Parmesan cheese Dash of black pepper

Whisk together olive oil, mustard, egg, anchovies, garlic, and shallots. Set dressing mixture aside. Toss romaine lettuce, seafood, and dressing together in a bowl. Top with a liberal sprinkling of Parmesan cheese and black pepper.

Yield: 8 servings.

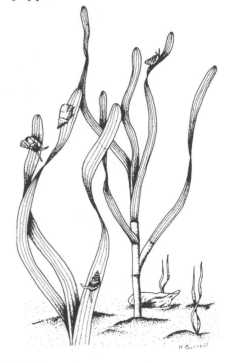

Main Dish

Seafood Quiche

1	pound crabmeat, bits of shell removed
¾	cup chopped cooked shrimp
2	eggs, beaten
¼	cup chopped celery
¼	cup chopped onion
¼	cup chopped green and/or red bell pepper
1	tablespoon Worcestershire sauce
¼	cup mayonnaise
⅛	cup all-purpose flour
1	deep-dish pie shell
½	pound process cheese, cubed
⅛	teaspoon seafood seasoning

Combine first 10 ingredients. Place one-third crab mixture into pie shell; add half of cheese. Top with one-third crab mixture; add remaining cheese, and top with remaining one-third crab mixture. Sprinkle seafood seasoning lightly on top of quiche. Bake at 350° for 45 minutes (test center of quiche for doneness). Let stand 10 minutes before serving. Great with cornbread and coleslaw.

Yield: 6 servings.

Off Loading Fish

CHESAPEAKE BAY

Main Dish

Crab-and-Shrimp Quiche

1	teaspoon all-purpose flour
1	teaspoon mayonnaise
4	eggs, beaten
3	ounces beer
1	pint half-and-half
1	cup fresh or canned crabmeat, bits of shell removed
1	cup fresh or canned shrimp
½	pound shredded sharp Cheddar cheese
½	pound shredded Swiss cheese
2	(8-inch) pie crusts

Combine first 9 ingredients, and pour into pie crusts. Bake at 300° for 1½ hours.

Yield: 6 to 8 servings.

Main Dish

Lobster-and-Salmon Tamale

3   ounces lobster meat
9   ounces salmon scraps or belly meat
12 ounces fresh salmon
¾   teaspoon salt
1   egg, beaten
4   tablespoons butter or margarine, finely cubed

⅓   cup coarsely chopped fresh cilantro
1   tablespoon finely chopped serrano chile
2   tablespoons whipping cream
8-10 large dried cornhusks, soaked in hot water until pliable

Parboil lobster about 3 minutes, or until less than half cooked; cool. Cut lobster and salmon scraps into ½-inch pieces, and set aside. Puree salmon with salt and egg in a food processor. In a bowl set over ice and water, mix puree with diced lobster and salmon, butter, cilantro, serrano, and cream. Divide mixture evenly between the cornhusks; roll and tie tamales. Steam 8 minutes. Cool slightly, and serve with jalapeño sauce or green chile sauce. Serve with boiled corn and a salad.

Yield: 8 to 10 tamales.

Chefs' Menus

Berret's, which opened in the early 1980's, is a superb addition to Merchant's Square in Williamsburg. Students and local residents enjoy the fresh seafood dishes and the fine reputation Berret's has earned. During the winter, the hearty seafood soups and open fire provide a warm welcome; and in good weather, a crowd can always be found at the outdoor raw bar.

BERRET'S
199 South Boundary Street - Merchant Square
Williamsburg, VA 23185-4049

For reservations call 757/253-1847

River's Inn opened in May of 1996 and is located on historic Sarah's Creek. The Gloucester Point shore near Sarah's Creek remained a heavily wooded area that belonged chiefly to such nearby plantations as Little England and Rosewell until after World War I. It was originally called Tyndall's Point, after an early explorer who mapped Virginia's shores. A ferry operated there during most of Virginia's existence, because the distance from Yorktown to Gloucester Point represents the shortest distance of any crossing on the lower river.

The town of Gloucester grew up on the cliff and the beachfront between Gloucester Point and Sarah's Creek, but it dwindled in the 19th and 20th centuries. The area was taken by Cornwallis' army in 1781 and fortified against American and French attacks, which never occurred. Some trenches and fortifications were re-dug by the Confederates in 1861-65 in hopes of stopping federal ships from penetrating the York in the Peninsula campaign, but the fort evidently had little effect.

Sarah's Creek in earlier times harbored fishing and oystering businesses and a number of small wooden shipbuilding plants. Since the creation of York River Yacht Haven, in the post-World War II era, it has become the home port for hundreds of pleasure boats. Visible in the trees across the creek facing the marina is the beautiful 18th-century mansion, Little England, built by the Perrin family.

Dining at River's Inn
Gloucester Point, Virginia

*Come enjoy a delicious meal at the River's Inn on Sarah's Creek
Site of the York River Yacht Haven.*

RIVER'S INN
*8109 Yacht Haven Drive
Gloucester Point, VA 23062*

For reservations call 804/642-9942

BERRET'S AND RIVER'S INN
Chef Richard Carr

Menu

*Pan Smoked Mountain Trout
with Baby Lettuces, Heirloom Tomatoes, Mozzarella
Cheese and River's Inn Vinaigrette Dressing*

Chesapeake Bay Jambalaya

*Pan Seared Sea Scallops with Shiitake Mushroom
Sauce, Puff Pastry and Sweet Bell Peppers*

Crab Feast at River's Inn -
Gloucester Point, Virginia

Pan Smoked Mountain Trout with Baby Lettuces, Heirloom Tomatoes, Mozzarella Cheese and River's Inn Vinaigrette Dressing

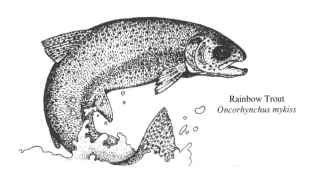

Rainbow Trout
Oncorhynchus mykiss

2	cups assorted baby lettuces, such as radicchio, maché, etc.		Vegetable oil or spray
1	(10-ounce) deboned fresh rainbow trout	½	cup sliced fresh mozzarella cheese
	Dash salt	2	medium heirloom tomatoes, sliced
	Dash pepper	¼	cup River's Inn vinaigrette dressing (substitute an herb vinaigrette)
	Dash sugar		
	Wood chips		

Clean the baby lettuces and drain the water very well; refrigerate. Take the rainbow trout, wash thoroughly and pat dry. Sprinkle with the salt, pepper and sugar. Heat a cast iron skillet on high heat until very hot, then add the soaked wood chips with a little bit of water so chips will smoke. Place an open grill over the wood chips. Spray grill with vegetable oil spray or rub with vegetable oil and place fish with flesh side down, pointed toward the chips. Cover the grill with a dome and capture as much smoke as possible over the fish. Cook for approximately 5 minutes. Arrange the lettuces, cheese and tomatoes on a chilled plate, place warm fish over and drizzle with vinaigrette. Serve immediately.

Yield: 2 servings.

Chesapeake Bay Jambalaya

2	tablespoons olive oil
1	tablespoon garlic puree
1	stalk celery, cut bias
3	yellow onions, julienned
2	bay leaves
1	tablespoon dried oregano
1	teaspoon salt
1	teaspoon white pepper
1	teaspoon black pepper
1	teaspoon red pepper
1	teaspoon thyme leaves
1	teaspoon basil leaves
1	teaspoon paprika
1	cup water
2	chicken bouillon cubes
½	gallon diced fresh tomatoes
½	cup tomato paste
	Dash sugar, optional
4	(3-ounce) rockfish fillets
1	cup smoked Surry sausage, sliced
12	littleneck clams
16	oysters, freshly shucked
4	(3-ounce) grilled duck breasts
1	cup yellow peppers, julienned
1	cup green peppers, julienned
1	cup red peppers, julienned

In a stockpot place olive oil, garlic, celery and onions and sauté until hot. Add the bay leaves, oregano, salt, white pepper, black pepper, red pepper, thyme, basil and paprika to the stock pot and reduce heat to medium. Add the water, bouillon cubes and tomatoes and bring back to a boil. Add the tomato paste,

(Continued on next page)

(Chesapeake Bay Jambalaya, continued)

reduce heat and simmer. At this point, remove a small amount of the sauce, cool and taste to make sure the flavors are balanced. A small amount of sugar may need to be added. When the sauce is complete, add the rockfish fillets, sausage and clams. Continue to cook on simmer and cover. When the clams open and the fish is thoroughly cooked, add oysters, grilled duck breast, and bell peppers, remove from heat, and leave partially covered. When ready to serve, place a cup of cooked rice in a bowl and portion the seafood and meats around the rice, and serve with a large spoon.

Yield: 4 servings.

Pan Seared Sea Scallops with Shiitake Mushroom Sauce, Puff Pastry and Sweet Bell Peppers

1	(5 x 5-inch) square sheet puff pastry, cut in half diagonally	1/4	pound sea scallops (approximately 5-6)
1	cup heavy cream	1	tablespoon white wine
1/2	cup sliced shiitake mushrooms	1	tablespoon red sweet bell peppers
1/4	teaspoon seafood bouillon (substitute chicken if necessary)	1	tablespoon green sweet bell peppers
1/2	tablespoon fine chopped parsley	1	tablespoon yellow sweet bell peppers
	Vegetable oil		

Cook the puff pastry at instructed time and temperature and set aside. In a saucepan, place heavy cream, shiitake mushrooms and bouillon. Cook at medium-high temperature until boiling, simmer until reduced by half. Add chopped parsley and remove from heat. Using a separate sauté pan, heat to a very high temperature, and coat with a small amount of vegetable oil. Place scallops down into the pan, searing the meat on both sides. Reduce heat and add the wine and bell peppers. On a plate open up the puff pastry, removing the top. Pour the shiitake mushroom sauce over the bottom of pastry. Place the scallops over the sauce, and arrange the top of the puff pastry off to the side of bottom pastry. Garnish with peppers.

Yield: 1 serving.

Chef Jimmy Sneed and his partner, Adam Steely, opened The Frog and the Redneck, in Richmond, Va. in April of 1993. Only six months after opening, The Frog and the Redneck was acclaimed by *Esquire Magazine* as "one of the Best New Restaurants in America." It has since been written about in *Gourmet, Bon Appétit, Southern Living, USA Today,* the *New York Times,* and numerous other national and local publications. *The Washington D.C. Zagat Guide* writes that The Frog and the Redneck is "worth going the hundred miles to Richmond to taste the 'amazing' things Jimmy does with regional products." Prior to coming to Richmond, Jimmy first earned a national reputation based on his unadulterated preparation of stunning local product while working at Windows on Urbanna Creek in Urbanna, Va.

Jimmy's first true culinary initiation came while preparing for international law in Paris, in 1974. He had taken a job at Le Cordon Bleu cooking school translating for the American students. It was there that he was exposed to the philosophy of 'Grande Cuisine' and the respect with which great chefs treat their product.

After a year in Paris, Jimmy returned to the United States and pursued a career in cooking. Frustrated by the level of cuisine to which he was exposed, he eventually sought a mentor to teach him about great food. Luck was with him, as he spent the next seven years learning from two of the greatest chefs in America, Jean-Louis Palladin and Guenther Seeger.

The "Frog" of The Frog and the Redneck is meant, in general, as a tribute to what the French have contributed to modern cuisine and, specifically, to what Chef Palladin taught Jimmy. "He made me a chef," says Jimmy.

Jimmy was chosen by Julia Child as a featured chef in her recent series "in Julia's Kitchen with Master Chefs." (Julia later attended a dinner in her honor at the restaurant.) He has also appeared on CNN, the Discovery Channel's "Great American Chefs" series, and The Television Food Network, among others. Jimmy was nominated in 1995 and 1996, for a James Beard Award for "Best

American Chef" in the Mid-Atlantic region. He is a frequent contributor to several major publications that include *Fine Cooking, Restaurant Hospitality* and *Washingtonian*; in addition, Jimmy writes a lighthearted, sometimes irreverent newsletter for the restaurant.

Jimmy is a regularly featured guest chef/lecturer at L'Acadamie de Cuisine in Maryland. In addition, he has taught at Le Cordon Bleu in Ottawa, lectured at the Smithsonian Institute and taught a culinary arts course at The College of William and Mary.

Located at 1423 East Cary Street in historic Shockoe Slip,
The Frog and the Redneck is housed in a warehouse built around 1875.
Cartoon murals by Happy the Artist, neon artwork and upbeat music
create a comfortable atmosphere for the enjoyment of great food.

THE FROG AND THE REDNECK
1423 East Cary Street
Richmond, VA 23219

For reservations call 804/648-FROG

THE FROG AND THE REDNECK
Chef Jimmy Sneed

Menu

Sweet Red Pepper Soup

*Fresh Mustard Pasta
with Red and Yellow Peppers, Fresh Spinach,
Calamata Olives and Fresh Grilled Shrimp*

Warm Chocolate Gooey Thing

Sweet Red Pepper Soup

6	red peppers	Sea salt
1	quart heavy cream	

Split the peppers in half and remove the seeds. Cut into quarters and put into a pan. Add the cream and simmer until peppers are soft (6-8 minutes). Blend in blender or food processor. Add salt to taste. Return to stove and heat to a simmer. Serve in a hot soup plate and sprinkle with fresh chopped chives or fresh lump crabmeat.

Yield: 6 servings.

The sea salt is what makes the soup sweet.

Fresh Mustard Pasta with Red and Yellow Peppers, Fresh Spinach, Calamata Olives and Fresh Grilled Shrimp

2	tablespoons extra-virgin olive oil	2	quarts fresh spinach (picked and washed)
2	red peppers (cored, seeded and julienned)	2	quarts cooked homemade pasta
		3	tablespoons butter
2	yellow peppers (cored, seeded and julienned)	10	Calamata olives (pitted and quartered)
	Sea salt	36	(15-20 count) shrimp (6 per person)
	Freshly ground black pepper		Flour
6	ounces chicken stock	½	cup olive oil or clarified butter

Sauté the peppers in the olive oil over medium-high heat. Season the peppers with salt and pepper as they cook. When the peppers are soft, add the stock, spinach and pasta. Heat these ingredients, tossing occasionally. Remove from the heat and add the cold butter, always moving as it melts. Add the olives, salt and pepper to taste.

Peel and devein the shrimp. Season both sides with salt and pepper and dredge in flour; shake off excess flour. Heat olive oil or butter in a large skillet. Add the shrimp, cooking each side for about 45 seconds. Remove and arrange on top of the pasta.

Mustard Pasta Dough

1	cup white flour
1	cup semolina flour
4	egg yolks
	Sea salt
	Freshly ground black pepper
1	tablespoon dry mustard
1	tablespoon Meaux mustard (or hearty country style)
3-4	plastic coat hangers
1	quart stock
¼	pound cold butter, cut into chunks

To prepare the dough, mix flour, eggs, salt and pepper together to make the pasta dough. You can do this by hand, with a mixer paddle, or with a dough blade in your food processor. It should have a fairly firm consistency and should not be sticky to the touch. Add more flour if too sticky, more egg if too dry. To add the mustard, knead dry mustard and meaux mustard into the dough. You need not be too thorough since it will spread itself through the pasta as you roll it out. Dust the dough with flour and wrap in plastic. Refrigerate for an hour or more allowing the gluten in the flour to relax. The dough is now ready to use, and will keep in the refrigerator for a day or so but will discolor if left longer - you are safer to freeze it if the wait is longer than 12 hours. To roll out the dough, cut the dough into 4 pieces and, one at a time, roll them through the widest setting of the pasta machine. Fold each piece over and flour the outside lightly. Continue rolling it through the machine, flouring lightly each time. Do this 6 or 7 times until the dough is a neat, smooth rectangle with even edges and a uniform color. Then, always flouring the dough, pass it through the rollers several times without folding, setting the rollers to a thinner setting each time the dough goes through. Continue rolling out to the desired thinness. To cut the dough by hand, dust the sheet of dough liberally on both sides with flour. Now roll it up upon itself, and it must not stick to itself - more flour is safer than less! Start at one end, fold an inch of the dough over

(Continued on next page)

(Mustard Pasta Dough, continued)

upon itself and continue folding until you can roll it up into a long tube. Using a very sharp knife, cut the tube into crosswise slices about ⅛-inch thick. Pick up the strips, shake them out, and drape them onto coat hangers. If you have a pasta machine, follow the machine directions for cutting the pasta. To cook, bring the stock to a boil and stir in the pasta, cover briefly and bring back to a boil. Then uncover and boil slowly, tasting almost continually until it is just cooked through. (Fresh made pasta may take only a few seconds, while dried pasta can take several minutes.) When ready, lift it out with a pasta fork into a wide pan, not draining too thoroughly - you need a bit of liquid to form the sauce. Taste, and correct seasoning, then turn the heat on to high. Add the cold butter and swirl the pan around by its handle, tossing the pasta until the butter emulsifies into a creamy sauce. Serve immediately.

Yield: 6 servings.

When making the dough, try adding one of the following ingredients in place of the mustard. Black pepper pasta - add 1½ teaspoons freshly ground black pepper; chive pasta - add 3 tablespoons minced chives; paprika pasta - add 3 tablespoons paprika powder; curry pasta - add 1 tablespoon curry powder; saffron pasta - add a pinch of saffron steeped in water (for coloring and flavoring).

VIMS Student with a Striped Bass

Warm Chocolate Gooey Thing

7	ounces semi-sweet chocolate
7	ounces unsalted butter
5	eggs
5	ounces confectioner's sugar
2	ounces cake flour

Melt the chocolate and butter in a double boiler over moderate heat. Remove from the boiler and whisk to combine. Whip the eggs until tripled in volume, then fold the eggs into the chocolate mixture. Sift the sugar and flour into the chocolate and combine thoroughly. Line two small Pyrex cups with jumbo cup cake liners and fill equally with the mixture. Bake them in a 400° oven for 10 minutes, then remove to a cooling rack. After ½ hour, unmold them upside down on to plates and serve with freshly whipped cream and chocolate sauce. You can also bake the cakes earlier and microwave them individually for about ten seconds to soften the liquid center. You may wish to do a test batch in your oven because a slight variance in oven temperature may cause them to overcook.

CHOCOLATE SAUCE:

10	ounces semi-sweet chocolate
1	cup cream

Melt chocolate and cream in a double boiler, whisking together until smooth. The sauce will stay as liquid at room temperature.

Yield: 7 servings.

THE KITCHEN AT POWHATAN PLANTATION

Powhatan Plantation is situated on 256 of the original 1,000 acres deeded to Mr. Richard Taliaferro in the early 1700's. The plantation and The Kitchen sit amidst the colonial history and beauty so typical of the Williamsburg area.

In 1735, Richard Taliaferro, then Williamsburg's leading architect and builder, constructed Powhatan's Manor House as his residence. It is now the hallmark of Powhatan Resort. Restored and furnished with painstaking attention to historical details, the Manor House appears on both the Virginia and National Registers as a historical landmark.

The plantation kitchen is a separate building as was the practice during Colonial times to prevent the possibility of fire in the Manor House. It has been carefully restored to its original appearance and transformed into The Kitchen at Powhatan Plantation. The random width pine flooring accents the Habersham reproductions and 18th century antiques that comprise the dining tables and support furniture. Additional care was given to the appointments, accessories, and table place settings. China, crystal and white linen dress each table. Pewter is used just as it was when the original property owner entertained George Washington and Patrick Henry in the Manor House. Employees, dressed in colonial attire, are well versed in the plantation's history and are happy to answer your questions.

Blending the atmosphere of the 18th century with American regional cuisine makes The Kitchen a unique dining experience. The menus change frequently to provide our diners with the freshest local and regional products during the peak of their season. With all respects to the contemporary diner's diet, we use only grapeseed, canola and virgin olive oils for sautéeing and salad dressings, coupled with heart-healthy methods of preparation.

Our wine list represents selections from Europe and North America. This offers our diners a wide range of wines from which to choose a compliment to their meal. We are very proud of our Zinfandel selection...a true American varietal.

Come...join us for a most memorable evening.

THE KITCHEN AT POWHATAN PLANTATION
3601 Ironbound Road
Williamsburg, VA 23188

For reservations call 757/220-1200, ext. 708

DIRECTOR OF FOOD AND BEVERAGE
C. Meredith Nicolls, Jr.

CHEF DE CUISINE
Christine Zambito

Menu

*Conch with Fresh Tagliolene, Garlic, Thyme
and White Wine*

*Octopus Salad with Fennel, Black Olives,
Arugula and Lemon Oil*

*Pan Seared Skate with Sweet Potato Puree
and Caper Brown Butter Sauce*

Bread Pudding

Tonging for Oysters

Conch with Fresh Tagliolene, Garlic, Thyme and White Wine

5	pounds conch		1/4	cup chopped garlic
3	cups dry white wine		1	cup dry white wine
2	bunches thyme		2	tablespoons thyme, chopped
1/4	cup garlic cloves		2	tablespoons butter, unsalted
1/4	cup vegetable or olive oil			Fresh black pepper

The conch must be rinsed well in cold water before cooking. Put the conch in a pot and cover with fresh cold water. Cook slowly over medium heat for 2 to 3 hours, adding water if necessary. Cool. With cocktail fork remove conch meat from shell and set aside. Decant cooking liquid slowly and reserve. (There will be a lot of sand on the bottom.) Put conch meat in a clean pot with 3 cups dry white wine, 2 bunches of thyme, 1/4 cup garlic and enough water to cover. Cook over medium heat until tender. (This should be about 45 minutes to one hour.) Add the reserved cooking liquid if needed. Remove the conch meat and strain liquid through a fine strainer. Reserve. Dice conch into small pieces. Reserve. In a sauté pan over medium heat, heat olive oil or vegetable oil. Add chopped garlic and cook until it just begins to brown. Add diced conch, 1 cup white wine, 2 tablespoons chopped thyme and 1-2 cups reserved cooking liquid (from the second cooking of the conch). Simmer 5 minutes. Add butter and fresh black pepper. Toss with tagliolene or pasta of your choice.

Tagliolene

2	cups semolina flour		3	eggs
1 1/2	cups all-purpose flour		1	tablespoon olive oil
1/2	teaspoon salt		2	tablespoons water

Mix dry ingredients in a large mixing bowl and form a well. Add liquid ingredients to well and stir together to form a stiff dough. Knead about 2-3 minutes by hand or with a doughhook or mixer. Add water or flour if needed. Wrap dough and let rest at least 30 minutes (can rest overnight if needed). Cut dough into small pieces and roll through pasta machine to desired shape and thickness. (Tagliolene is technically the finest pasta noodle.)

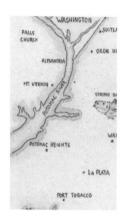

Braised Octopus

5	pounds octopus
2	tablespoons oil
2	teaspoons salt
1	tablespoon black peppercorns
1	medium onion diced
3	stalks celery, sliced
3	large carrots, sliced
2	tablespoons garlic cloves
1	tablespoon dry thyme
2	bay leaves
2	cups dry red wine
2	cups dry white wine
	Water

Rinse octopus well. Cut off legs and cut into individual pieces. Remove head pocket and cut into 2-3 pieces. In a large sauce pan heat oil. Add octopus and sear well over medium heat 5-10 minutes. Add salt and pepper. Add vegetables and herbs and stir frequently for 10 minutes. Add red and white wine and enough water to just cover octopus. Simmer, stirring occasionally, for 1½ hours or until the octopus is tender. Remove octopus and strain liquid through a fine strainer. Store octopus in liquid until ready to use.

Octopus Salad

2	medium fennel bulbs, shaved
¼	cup Calamata olives, sliced
3	cups arugula
1	cup octopus, thin sliced
¼	cup lemon oil
	Salt to taste
	Pepper to taste

Toss together all ingredients except octopus, arrange octopus on top and serve.

Pan Seared Skate with Caper Brown Butter Sauce

1	tablespoon vegetable oil	⅔	cup butter
4	(6-8 ounce) skate wing pieces (on bone or fillets)	3	tablespoons capers
	Salt	1	tablespoon lemon juice
	Pepper	1	tablespoon chopped parsley

In a large sauté pan, heat oil over high heat. Season skate with salt and pepper. Place skate in pan thin side first (if on bone) or ribbed side first (if fillet). Cook 2-3 minutes and then flip over carefully. Cook 2-3 more minutes. Remove from pan (if on the bone, continue cooking in oven 5 minutes at 400°). Add butter to hot pan and let melt. Begin to brown, stirring constantly. Once butter is brown add the rest of the ingredients. Add salt and pepper to taste. Serve sauce over skate wing.

Yield: 4 servings.

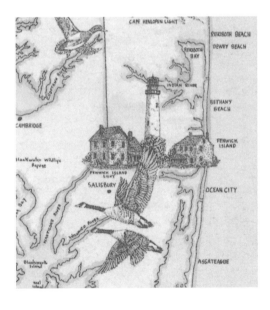

Sweet Potato Puree

4	large sweet potatoes, peeled and cut in chunks
1	Idaho potato
	Salt to taste
4	tablespoons butter
4	tablespoons brown sugar
	Fresh nutmeg

Cook sweet potatoes and Idaho potato in cold water until soft. Drain well and return to pot. Return pot to stove on low heat to dry out potatoes slightly. Mash potatoes through food mill or ricer, or with mixer. Add the rest of the ingredients and mix well.

Yield: 4-6 servings.

Bread Pudding with Currants and Pecans

6	cups diced bread (not stale)
2	cups heavy cream
5	eggs
1	cup sugar
1	teaspoon cinnamon
1	teaspoon vanilla
1/4	cup water
1/2	cup pecans
1/2	cup dry currants

Cut bread and set aside. Mix together cream and eggs until well blended. Add sugar, cinnamon, vanilla and water. Mix well. In a large bowl mix together egg mixture, bread, pecans and currants until well mixed. Grease a 9 x 9 inch square or 9 inch round pan well. Preheat over to 350°. Continue to mix bread until soaked and liquid is all absorbed. Turn into greased pan. Cover with foil and bake 35-45 minutes or until set. Remove foil and sprinkle top with granulated sugar and bake 15 more minutes. Serve warm with whipped cream or ice cream.

Yield: 8-12 servings.

the Lucky Star

From the airy peach and sand colors in the intimate dining room, to the just-picked taste and texture of the food, the 8-year-old Lucky Star radiates freshness. Chef and co-owner Amy Brandt is changing her menu every two or three weeks if that is what's needed to take advantage of the plethora of vegetables, seafood and meats available in eastern Virginia. And you can be sure her weekly specials will resonate with the pick of the crop. "What comes through that door had better be the best," said Brandt, talking about the food supplied to her by local farmers and fishermen. "Our success lies in the consistency of the quality of the product and the presentation," she said. An example of specials may include an appetizer of grilled calamari over sliced tomatoes, Vidalia onions and fresh basil with a sherry vinaigrette, and an entrée of herb-roasted pork loin chop served over a sauté of tomatoes, garlic, herbs, Calamata olives and angel-hair pasta. "I want the customer to look at the menu and say, 'Gee, I never thought about putting those things together.' " Brandt said.

Brandt came to cooking via her French/Swiss parents. "They were very food-oriented," she said. "Not haute cuisine, more country-style food, European food." Her parents' interest in food, coupled with her own passion for art - she paints when she's not cooking - lends her culinary work, a flow and color not present in all dining experiences. Brandt graduated from the Rhode Island campus of Johnson & Wales University, College of Culinary Arts. Her experience there was the first time she'd worked in a professional kitchen. These days, her domain is the kitchen, while her partner, Butch Butt, manages the restaurant and wait staff.

And the name Lucky Star? "It just seemed everything fell into place for us to start this place," Brandt said, gesturing around the restaurant. "It was like we were under our lucky star." Excerpted from Debra Gordon at the *Virginian-Pilot*.

THE LUCKY STAR
1608 Pleasure House Road
Virginia Beach, VA 23455

To make reservations call 757/363-8410

Chef Amy Brandt

Menu

*Jumbo Lump Crabmeat
and Baked Asparagus Salad*

*Sautéed Tuna with
Tomato Black Olive Sauce*

*Fall Apple Golden Raisin
and Black Walnut Crisp*

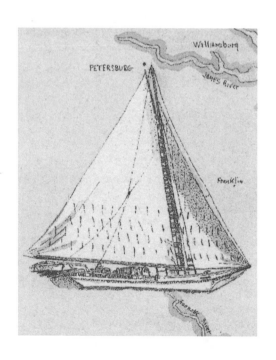

Jumbo Lump Crabmeat and Baked Asparagus Salad

2 pounds asparagus, peeled if necessary
1 tablespoon fruity olive oil
1 pinch kosher salt
1 pinch coarsely ground black pepper
¼ pound prosciutto, sliced very thin

½ pound mesclun greens
1 pound lump crabmeat
½ cup lemon juice
1 cup olive oil
¼ pound hard Parmesan cheese, shaved

Preheat oven to 425°. Place the peeled asparagus in an oven proof pan. Drizzle with the olive oil and season with the salt and pepper. Cover with aluminum foil and bake approximately 15 minutes or until asparagus is tender. Uncover and refrigerate to cool. Assemble the plates by laying out the sliced prosciutto, place the asparagus on the prosciutto. Lay the greens at the bottom of the asparagus spears. Place the crabmeat on the greens. Whisk together the lemon juice and olive oil. Drizzle the salad with the lemon dressing and garnish with the shaved Parmesan.

Yield: 6 servings.

Sautéed Tuna with Tomato Black Olive Sauce

SAUCE:

¼	cup olive oil
6	cloves garlic, sliced
1	yellow onion, peeled and diced
36	Calamata olives, pitted and chopped
4	cups canned tomatoes, crushed
8	Roma tomatoes, large diced
2	tablespoons tomato puree
½	cup shrimp stock
½	cup chicken stock
½	cup white wine
¼	teaspoon crushed red pepper flakes
2	teaspoons fresh sage, chopped
2	teaspoons fresh marjoram, chopped
½	cup fresh parsley, chopped
½	cup lemon juice

TUNA STEAKS:

4	(8-ounce) tuna steaks
	Kosher salt
	Black pepper, freshly ground
2	tablespoons olive oil
¼	cup white wine
1	tablespoon fresh parsley, roughly chopped
1	tablespoon fresh basil, roughly chopped

To make the sauce, heat a large heavy gauge saucepan. When hot, add the olive oil and garlic. Brown the garlic lightly. Add onion and sauté until soft. Add the remaining ingredients and stir to combine thoroughly. Cook about 30 minutes over medium high heat. The sauce should be slightly thickened when done. Season the tuna steaks with salt and pepper. Heat a heavy gauge sauté pan to medium high heat. When hot, add the oil and gently place the tuna in the pan and sear until browned. Turn and sear 1 minute, add wine and herbs. Cover and keep warm. Set pan aside from heat for 5 minutes. Tuna should finish cooking in this time. Serve on hot plates with garlic potatoes and the tomato sauce.

Yield: 4 servings.

Fall Apple Golden Raisin and Black Walnut Crisp

FILLING:

12	large Stayman or Rome apples	¾	cup flour
8	ounces golden raisins	½	cup brown sugar
2	lemons (juice and zest)		Fresh grated nutmeg
1	cup apple cider	½	teaspoon ground cinnamon

CRISP TOPPING:

2	cups all-purpose flour	1½	cups black walnuts
¾	cup brown sugar	¾	cup butter, room temperature
	Pinch salt		cut into cubes

Peel, core and cut apples into medium-sized pieces. Toss in a large bowl with the remaining filling ingredients. Place in baking dish - ceramic preferred. To make the topping, combine flour, brown sugar and salt in a separate bowl. Mix with a mixer on low. Add walnuts and butter and mix on medium until flour mixture and butter are combined but not pasty. Crumble topping over filling. Bake in preheated oven at 375° for 45 minutes or until browned.

Yield: 8-10 servings.

Sage's Bistro was taken over by Tom '81 and Theresa Franco in the fall of 1996. It is a beautiful restaurant which was built in the summer of 1995. Decorated by Collaborative designs, Sage's Bistro has accents of Italian tile, marble and handpainted frescos. With two levels of dining accented by wrought iron railings and white tablecloths, many have labeled Sage's as one of the most beautiful restaurants in the area.

Chef Robert Holt, who trained under Jerry Bryant at the Coastal Grill, carefully plans each menu item which can be classified as contemporary American cuisine with an International flair. Mike Harr, the Sous Chef, is one of the area's most exciting young chefs and is a recent graduate of Johnson and Wales.

In the short span since the Franco's ownership, Sage's has garnished two impressive reviews from *Portfolio Magazine* and *The Virginian-Pilot*. Among its list of honors, Sage's holds the Three Diamond Award and a Golden Fork Award, which acknowledge the best restaurants in the Hampton Roads area.

After graduating from the College of William and Mary in May of 1981, Tom Franco decided to pursue the restaurant business. His first assignment took him to Orlando where he managed a restaurant at the Church Street Station. After Orlando, Franco headed west to Colorado. And after five years of managing restaurants in Colorado, Franco, with his wife, Theresa, opened what was to be their first of three restaurants. Cafe Alpine, located in Breckenridge, Colorado opened in 1992. Four years later in Corolla, North Carolina, the Franco's opened Grouper's Grill. And in the fall of 1996, Sage's Bistro came under Tom and Theresa's ownership.

Tom and Theresa Franco have stopped moving and plan to call Hampton Roads their home. After moving 13 times in the last 12 years, the Franco's are finally staying put. As Theresa puts it, "being with Tom is like being married to someone in the military without all the benefits!" But then she adds with a smile, "the last 12 years have been anything but boring!"

SAGE'S BISTRO
1658 Pleasure House Road - Thoroughgood Commons
Virginia Beach, VA 23455

For reservations call 757/460-1691

OWNERS
Tom '81 & Theresa Franco

CHEF DE CUISINE
Robert Holt

SOUS CHEF
Mike Harr

Menu

Tuna Sashimi

*Spinach Salad
with a Mango - Pecan Vinaigrette*

*Pan Seared Scallops with Shiitake,
Leek and Sundried Tomato Cream Sauce*

Pan Seared Red Snapper

Tuna Sashimi

1   **Sushi tuna**
¼   **cup blackening spice**
    Greens or salad mix

WASABI SAUCE:
    Dry wasabi mix
    Water
    Chopped garlic
    Chopped ginger
    Rice wine vinegar
    Soy sauce

Coat tuna with blackening spice. Pan sear on all sides just to blacken, then set aside. Slice tuna sashimi very thin. To make wasabi dipping sauce, mix together the dry wasabi mix together with just enough water to make a paste. Whisk together garlic, ginger, rice wine vinegar and soy sauce. Serve the sashimi tuna over the greens with the wasabi dipping sauce.

Yield: 4 servings.

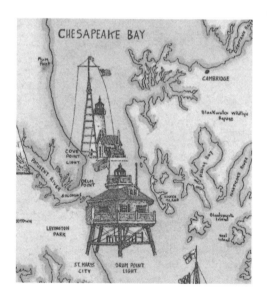

Spinach Salad with a Mango - Pecan Vinaigrette

¼   cup mango puree
¼   cup apple cider vinegar
2   tablespoons raspberry vinegar
1   tablespoon brown sugar
1   tablespoon Dijon mustard
½   cup olive oil

Dash salt
Dash pepper
2   bags picked and washed spinach
¼   cup goat cheese, crumbled
¼   cup spiced pecans

In a bowl whisk together the mango puree, apple and raspberry vinegar, brown sugar and mustard. Slowly incorporate the olive oil to make an emulsion. Season with salt and pepper. Toss the spinach in the vinaigrette and place nicely onto two plates. Decorate with the goat cheese and the spiced pecans.

Yield: 2 servings.

Pan Seared Scallops with Shiitake, Leek and Sundried Tomato Cream Sauce

3	scallops, cleaned and sliced in half
1	tablespoon chopped garlic
1	tablespoon chopped shallots
1/8	cup julienned leeks
1/8	cup julienned shiitakes
	Pinch sundried tomatoes, julienne
1/4	cup white wine
	Pinch basil, chiffanade
1/4	cup cream
	Dash salt
	Dash pepper

In a sauté pan, sear scallops until golden brown. Add garlic, shallots and sauté well. Add the leeks, shiitakes and sundried tomatoes. De-glaze mixture with white wine and then add the basil and the cream. Reduce slightly and season with salt and pepper.

Yield: 1 serving.

Pan Seared Red Snapper

¼	cup peanut oil	1	tablespoon chopped garlic
12	ounces red snapper	1	tablespoon basil, chiffanade
4	cups corn	2	tablespoons butter
1	cup diced red pepper		Dash salt
1	cup diced green pepper		Dash pepper
6	ounces jumbo lump crabmeat, picked through		

Put half of the peanut oil in a sauté pan and heat oil until smoky. Add red snapper and sear on both sides. Turn down heat and cook until done. In another sauté pan, heat the remaining peanut oil and sauté the corn, red pepper and green pepper. Add the crab, garlic and basil to the pepper mixture. Season with butter, salt and pepper. Serve the red snapper over the sautéed pepper mix.

Yield: 2 servings.

Seafood Products

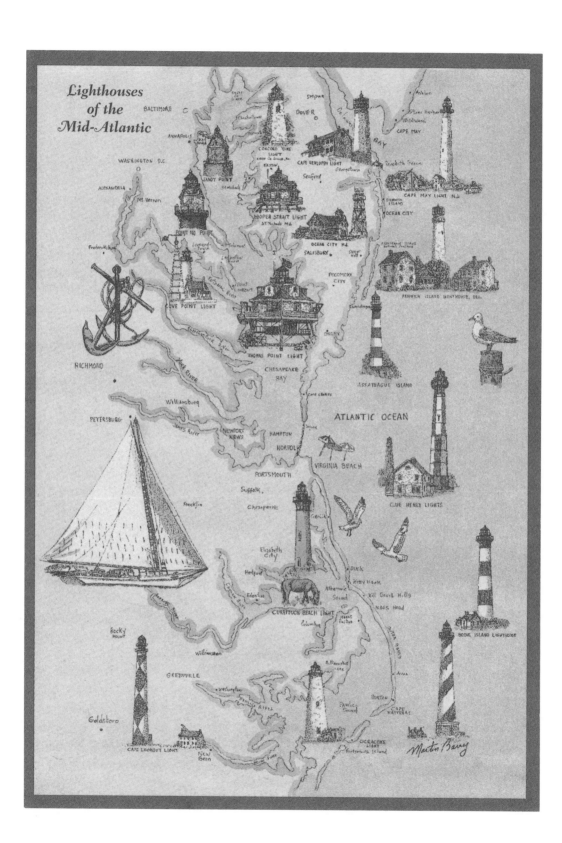

Lighthouses of the Mid-Atlantic

MID-ATLANTIC SEAFOOD FESTIVALS

Maryland

Maryland Office of Tourism Development
410/767-3400

APRIL

Nanticoke River Shad Festival
Shore of Nanticoke River
302/875-1650

MAY

From **May-September** the JOB Marketing and Travel Consultants hold weekly Seafood Feasts on Saturday and Sundays featuring gospel or party music in Baltimore City. For more information please call 888/375-0080 or in Baltimore call 410/581-0102.

Springfest
Ocean City
410/250-0125

The Lower Susquehanna History Festival
Port Deposit
410/378-2121

Music Crab Feast Picnic and Fireworks
Cockeysville
410/581-0102

Soft Shell Spring Fair
Crisfield
410/968-2500

JUNE

Queen Anne's County Waterman's Festival
Grasonville
410/643-5536

JULY

J. Millard Tawes Crab and Clam Bake
Crisfield
410/968-2500

AUGUST

Crab Days
St. Michaels
410/745-2916

Dorchester Chamber Seafood Fest-i-val
Cambridge
410/228-3575

Music Crab Feast Picnic and Fireworks
Cockeysville
410/581-0102

Havre de Grace Seafood Festival
Havre de Grace
410/939-2877

Rivertown Crab Feast and Festival
Port Deposit
410/378-2121

SEPTEMBER

Maryland Seafood Festival
Annapolis
410/268-7682

OCTOBER

Terrapin Sands Fish Fry
Crisfield
410/968-2500

Queen Anne's County Seafood Funfest
Stevensville
410/643-8530

J. Millard Tawes Oyster and Bull Roast
Crisfield
410/968-2501

St. Mary's County Oyster Festival
Leonardtown
301/863-5015

NOVEMBER

Oyster Fest
St. Michaels
410/745-2916

North Carolina

North Carolina Travel and Tourism Division
800/VISIT NC

MARCH

A Day at the Docks
Holden Beach
910/842-3828

APRIL

Grifton Shad Festival
Grifton
919/524-4356

Topsail Island Spring Fling
Surf City
910/328-4722

MAY

Tee & Sea Festival
Windsor
919/794-5302

Engelhard Seafood Festival
Engelhard
919/925-9461

JUNE

RiverFest
Plymouth
919/793-4804

AUGUST

Corolla Seafood Festival
Corolla
919/453-3242

Sneads Ferry Annual Shrimp Festival
Sneads Ferry
910/327-4911

SEPTEMBER

Crab & Art Festival
BelHaven
919/943-3770

OCTOBER

Annual NC Seafood Festival
Morehead City
919/726-6273

Annual NC Oyster Festival
Shallotte
910/754-6644

Fish Camp Jam
Gastonia
704/853-3474

Virginia

Virginia Tourism Corporation
800/VISIT VA
http://www.Virginia.org

MARCH

Bay Days
Richmond
804/367-6552
800/659-1727

APRIL

Shrimpfest
Salem
540/342-2640

Rappahanock Shad Festival
Fredericksburg
804/443-5629

MAY

Watermen's Heritage Weekend
Reedville
804/453-6529

Eastern Shore of Virginia Seafood Festival
Chincoteague
757/787-2460

June

Harborfest
Norfolk
757/627-5329

Annual Seawall Festival
Portsmouth
800/296-9933

Potomac River Festival
Colonial Beach
804/224-8145

Annual Bluefish Derby
Reedville
804/453-5325

Homestyle Music, Shrimp and Beef Festival
Chincoteague Island
757/336-6161

Bayou Boogaloo & Cajun Food Festival
Norfolk
757/441-2345

Northern Neck Seafood Festival
Windmill Point
804/435-1166

Summer Feast on the Square
Harrisonburg
540/434-2319

July

Seafood Fling at Fort Monroe
Hampton
757/727-3151

August

Beachfest
Fredericksburg
540/720-4871

SEPTEMBER

James River Fishing Jamboree
Scottsville
804/286-4800

Bay Seafood Festival
Kilmarnock
804/438-6268

Annual Hampton Bay Days
Hampton
757/727-6122

Northern Neck Seafood Extravaganza
Oak Grove
804/224-8687

Seafood Festival
Colonial Beach
804/224-8145

Fall Food Festival and Band Jam
Lynchburg
804/847-1499

A Taste of the Bay
Hampton
757/727-6122

OCTOBER

Eastern Shore of Virginia Harvest Festival
Kiptopeke
757/787-2460

Chincoteague Oyster Festival
Chincoteague Island
757/336-6161

Crabtown Festival of the Arts
Hampton
800/800-2202

NOVEMBER

Urbanna Oyster Festival
Urbanna

Reedville Oyster Roast
Reedville
804/453-6529

ACKNOWLEDGMENTS

EDITOR
The Wimmer Companies

FRONT COVER ARTIST
Martin Barry

LINE DRAWINGS & PHOTOGRAPHS
Provided by
Virginia Institute of Marine Science Publication Center

SECTION INTRODUCTIONS
Provided by
Vicki Clark
Marine Education Specialist
Sea Grant Marine Advisory Program
Virginia Institute of Marine Science

PROJECT COORDINATOR
Paula Hicks Mooradian M.B.A. '92

SOCIETY OF THE ALUMNI
W. Barry Adams
Jacqueline Genovese '87
Cindy Gillman
Alfred Jackson
John Jackson
Betty Vining

VIRGINIA INSTITUTE OF MARINE SCIENCE
Vicki Clark
Wanda Cohen
Kent Forrest
Susan Stein

RESTAURANTS

The Society of the Alumni wishes to express its appreciation
to these restaurants, inns and taverns for allowing us
to include their recipes in this book:

Berret's

Dynasty Restaurant

The Frog and the Redneck

The Kitchen at Powhatan Plantation

The Lucky Star

River's Inn

Sage's Bistro

REFERENCES

Boschung, Herbert T. Jr., Caldwell, David K., Caldwell, Melba C., et. al. 1983. *National Audubon Society Field Guide to North American Fishes, Whales, and Dolphins,* **Chanticleer Press, Inc., New York.**

Fontaine, Bertha V. And Turner, Sue. *Seafood Adventures from the Gulf and South Atlantic,* **Tampa, Florida: Gulf and South Atlantic Fisheries Development Foundation, Inc.**

Hicks, Doris. 1994. *A Consumer Guide to Safe Seafood Handling,* **Newark, Delaware: University of Delaware Sea Grant College Program.**

Skinner, Linda, ed. 1995. *The Complete Seafood Handbook,* **Portland, Maine: Journal Publications.**

INDIVIDUALS

Suzanne Allan

Katherine L. Atkins J.D. '92

Julie Down Bauer '95

Mildred F. Bell G.A. '70

Gem Blair-Elliot '79

Amy Brandt

Amelia Britt

Richard Carr

Huldah Champion '44

Vicki Clark

Tom David '74

Gloria M. Diggs

Sterry Kimball Davis '59

Betty Wrenn Day

Peggy Drake '72

Mary Cottrill Economou '77

Tom '81 and Theresa Franco

Dottie Nowland Gabig '61

Mark I. Ghorayeb '87

Anne S. Goldston M.D. '44

Teri Lattanze Gordon '86

Carol A. Gray

Velma Krowe Gray '65

Cindy Groman

Linda Lester Hagen '62

Kirk J. Havens

Kitty Dichtel Heffington '77

Nancy Sinclair Henry '62

Treazure P. Johnson '79

Jennifer L. C. H. Jones '96

Samuel H. Jones IV '96

Betty Joseph Kucewicz '63

Gini Anding La Charite '57

Grace Liu

Mary St. Thomas MacAdam '79

Leon McDaniel

Anne McGee '96

Marcie Mansfield

Marguerite Kelly Morris '65

Martha Mountain '86

Jim Newman '73

Scott Newton

Nancie L. Nichols M.Ed '78

June Joy Prah '39

Kim Rambow '90

Susan Rosenblatt '85

Gloria B. Rowe

J. Malcolm Shick B.S. '69, M.A. '71

Mary Mann Smith '73

Jimmy Sneed

Stephen H. Snell '66

Jeanne P. Snyder

Margie Brown Snyder '71

Hugh Stallworth M.B.A. '79

Tom '65 and Martha W. Steger '66

J. Michael Surface '75

Chuck Swaim '81

Virginia Van de Water D.Ed '88

Ginnie Peirce Volkman '64

Nancy Wagner '89

Fran Cunningham Ward C.A.S. '85

Ken Webb

Marti Welch

Jennifer Welham '90

Jane Yerkes

Index

WILLIAM & MARY BY THE SEA

ORDER FORM

Yes! I'd like more copies of WILLIAM & MARY BY THE SEA! Please send _____ copies of WILLIAM & MARY BY THE SEA for me and _____ copies for holiday gifts.

Total number of copies ordered _____ @ $16.93 per copy .... Subtotal = _____

Less 10% (7 or more copies) .... - _____

Virginia residents add 4.5% sales tax @ $. 76 per copy .... Subtotal = _____

Add $5 per address for 1-6 copies .... = _____

Add $8 per address for 7-12 copies .... = _____

TOTAL = _____

Name _____

Address _____

City _____ State _____ Zip _____

Daytime phone number _____

☐ Separate shipping information enclosed for additional addresses.

Payment information:

☐ Check enclosed (Make checks payable to *The Society of the Alumni*)

☐ Charge my ☐ MasterCard ☐ VISA

Account number _____ Expiration date _____

Signature _____

Mail to: The Alumni Gift Shop, The Society of the Alumni, P.O. Box 2100, Williamsburg, VA 23187-2100
To order by phone please call: 757/221-1170 or fax this form to 757/221-1186

- -

ORDER FORM

Yes! I'd like more copies of WILLIAM & MARY BY THE SEA! Please send _____ copies of WILLIAM & MARY BY THE SEA for me and _____ copies for holiday gifts.

Total number of copies ordered _____ @ $16.93 per copy .... Subtotal = _____

Less 10% (7 or more copies) .... - _____

Virginia residents add 4.5% sales tax @ $. 76 per copy .... Subtotal = _____

Add $5 per address for 1-6 copies .... = _____

Add $8 per address for 7-12 copies .... = _____

TOTAL = _____

Name _____

Address _____

City _____ State _____ Zip _____

Daytime phone number _____

☐ Separate shipping information enclosed for additional addresses.

Payment information:

☐ Check enclosed (Make checks payable to *The Society of the Alumni*)

☐ Charge my ☐ MasterCard ☐ VISA

Account number _____ Expiration date _____

Signature _____

Mail to: The Alumni Gift Shop, The Society of the Alumni, P.O. Box 2100, Williamsburg, VA 23187-2100
To order by phone please call: 757/221-1170 or fax this form to 757/221-1186